Magical
Kabbalah

Magical Kabbalah

Alan Richardson

Thoth Publications
Loughborough, United Kingdom

4th Edition
Copyright ©2006 Alan Richardson

A CIP catalogue record for this book is
available from the British Library.

Cover design by Helen Surman

ISBN-10   1-870450-53-1
ISBN-13   978-1-870450-53-9

Published by Thoth Publications
64 Leopold Street, Loughborough, LE11 5DN

Web address www.thoth.co.uk
email: enquiries@thoth.co.uk

Printed and bound in Great Britain

Contents

Introduction to the new and Final Edition

hen the Ancient Egyptians built new temples on the site of old, they deliberately retained aspects from the original for practical, symbolic, psychological and magical reasons. Likewise, over the past 30 years, this present book has gone through many changes over several editions in numerous languages, but has retained certain key-stones from its predecessors to help it all stand up, and give it a heritage.

The very first edition, entitled 'An Introduction to the Mystical Qabalah', presented itself at a very shallow intellectual level, which did no more than mirror my own state at the time. Mercifully a later edition with the same title managed to take on some depth, thanks to the prompting of certain 'inner contacts' which bothered me at the time; while the third version, called 'Magical Gateways', strove to present itself with some heart as well as mind, although it was pitched at the American market in obvious places. I only hope that this present version will sidestep the mind and heart, and manage to show some balls.

That first version was written when I was still a teenager, and I fancied that the book would sell hugely and enable me to buy a green open-topped Morgan sports car. Manchester United had just won the European Cup for the first time, and I was rubbing linseed oil on my upper lip in the belief that it might help my moustache grow. It didn't get published until 1974, when I was 22, though at least by that time my moustache and beard were fully developed. On the other hand I was also old enough and discriminating enough to feel exquisitely embarrassed by the dismal title, the dull cover, and what I felt were the juvenile attitudes on a topic that no more than a dozen people on the entire planet were interested in. There was no street cred in being a kabbalist back then. This was, of course, decades before every celebrity on the planet turned their egos and their cheque books toward the Kabbalah and its Mysteries.

My book was dedicated coyly to 'Bill for his immense help and kindness'. This was the legendary magician and kabbalist William G. Gray, whose biography I co-wrote with Marcus Claridge in 2003, entitled 'The Old Sod', and whose own writings on magic turned the whole art inside-out and upside down. On certain levels, this book still owes him an enormous debt. Whatever I know about the Kabbalah I learned from him. And he once told me, in his abrasive way, that if I *must* write books then at least I should try to make them original. I have always tried to do that, though sometimes it hasn't worked. If any reader finds the quirkiness of what follows a bit irritating then of course you should blame William G. Gray and not me. But stand on something to insulate you first.

Although Bill taught me many things in many ways at many levels over many years, it was actually the late, great Christine Hartley who *educated* me in magic, and whose biography I wrote as 'Dancers to the Gods'. If Bill Gray was a *real* Magician, then Christine was a truly *high* priestess, and an Adept if ever there was one. Whatever entities or energies have inspired the writing of this, are all down to her. That which lay behind Bill was far too austere and cerebral for me; but those other-dimensional beings which lay behind Christine Hartley welcomed me like an old friend - although they always kept me on my toes. As I have argued elsewhere, the world owes a huge debt to them both.

What I have tried to write is an introduction to the essentials of Magic, using the Kabbalah as a basis. It shows Magic to be a system of inner development which you can use to enhance your life, and the Kabbalah as a unique and infinitely flexible guru-free philosophy. The techniques given are tried and tested methods which will, in time, expand your consciousness. Whether you are a Christian, a Pagan, or something else, makes no difference. At the end of the book you will have the ability to make conscious links with what magicians call 'inner contacts', and which others call 'guides'. In truth, by virtue of the fact that few things ever happen in this business by chance, the very fact that you are reading this book at all means that those inner contacts are already paying a keen interest in your efforts. More importantly, you will also be left with ideas on how this Tradition may be developed in the decades to come, and of the part you might play.

The emphasis at all times is upon the individual, and on the effort that you as an individual must make. The study and practice of Magic as described herein requires no membership of any groups, no knowledge of ancient languages, and no worship of any individual, living or dead. I personally belong to no group, studied the peculiar philosophy of the Kabbalah for thirty years without ever once being able to recognise a single Hebrew letter, and have not found that my Magic has suffered in any way. And despite the mythological overtones, there is no essential religious element to the work, no requirement to believe in odd deities or worship the One God, no tedious morality or anti-morality. An atheist could adapt it all to his own terms of reference and still achieve radical transformation. An electrician could do similar. Just as we would not want other life-forms to worship us, the beings which lie behind our psyches want no holy obeisance sent toward them. That sort of thing is past. It is time we grew up. We must work with them - though respectfully - and have the sheer nerve to challenge them when necessary. Otherwise, we just become sheep.

This book is in fact simplistic, and deliberately so. Whether this is an excuse for my own shallowness, or a sincere attempt to get to the root of things, is something that you must decide for yourself. Sometimes, re-reading words that I wrote a lifetime ago, I can only shudder and think what a pompous, pretentious little bastard I was then. In a few places, as a kind of penance and exorcism, I've retained these paragraphs and quoted them back at myself with the option of being able to modify those opinions which seemed so obvious at the time.

Yet if there is anything good, wholesome or interesting about my life today, and if I have ever achieved anything unusual or original, then it is down to my life-long passion for Magic. Likewise, if I have managed to get through the dark times that we all experience, and come out of them with a bit more wisdom and tolerance, then it is entirely due to that same passion. Anyone who believes that Magic is pure escapism, knows nothing. We might as well criticise top-class athletes for taking up their sports in order to avoid the so-called 'realities' of life. We might as well criticise any human attempts at self-improvement in any sphere. It is sheer, unremitting effort. Which is why the old magicians called it The Work. No one works harder at life than the magician. You must strive by yourself and for yourself. Get books from the library by all means; buy a couple of recommended tomes and preferably tell all your friends to buy this one in large quantities. But if you try to achieve enlightenment by expensive residential courses run by those professional gurus who blight the Western world (and who knows how many inner worlds) by credit card enlightenment, then you're already missing the point.

Y'see the great magicians, the *real* magicians, all have full time jobs in the real world. The adepts of the legendary 'Hermetic Order of the Golden Dawn' which was founded in 1888, were doctors, teachers, artists, scientists, writers, colonels, astronomers, engineers, dramatists. The magical adepts or genuine witches *I* have met have been literary agents, nurses, electricians, writers, doctors, bus drivers, teachers, skin artists, dancers, chefs, or military men and women. To name but a very few professions. They all live and work in the real world. How else should it be?

Although the practice of Magic can enhance and transform your life, it is actually in the last conscious moments before death that it receives its full justification. We might call this the Parable of the Two Brothers (or Sisters!). One brother has no interest in Magic or any other spiritual system, and scorns it as mere escapism; the other works at Magic with all of his heart. At the moment before death, however, two distinctions occur, the *least* important being that the magician has actually got something to look forward to. (And if that proves to be false, as his scornful brother would insist, then after death it hardly matters anyway.) But the truly important distinction is in what the two have to look back upon. Both will have known love, sex, relationships, jobs, careers, profits and debts, laughter and sorrow and children and travel. The magician will have the full range of experience, the same intense memories as his sceptical brother but on top of these, in areas denied the latter, the magician will be able to look back also upon a life that extended through more than the usual dimensions. The magician will be able to look back upon inner experiences that were nothing less than... *extraordinary.*

In the practice of Magic, therefore, you will learn to link with energies and levels of consciousness that can transform you. These energies will come through in a perfectly natural way. In the magical scheme each individual consciousness is part of one great, corporate whole. We are one another, in fact. Changes within the heart and mind of the magician will eventually affect the heart and mind of the whole race. Each person must learn, therefore, that they have a responsibility to work Magic as brightly as they can. In a very true sense, the world, the future, depends upon it.

And the astonishing thing about magic is that it always works - though never *when* the newcomer wants, and rarely *how.* Rituals which I performed with specific intent in the mid-70s, for example, finally worked themselves through in the late 80s. Energies which I started working with (often in a bewildered way) in the 80s, are only now explaining themselves to me in this year of 2006. Older and just a teensy-bit wiser, these days, with grey streaks dignifying my facial hair, I can see that the timing has actually been perfect.

In the first stages of magical practice, as an intensely lonely youth (but which youth isn't?), I wanted nothing more than to join a group and be taken under the wing of some all-wise and all-knowing Adept. However, circumstances all seemed to conspire brilliantly against that possibility, so that I was always forced to work alone. The techniques and notions given herein, then, are essentially those which inspired my often inglorious but never fruitless early years, and which later on gave me the confidence to enter some strange and luminous realms indeed. I never became a great magician. I cannot claim that even now, nearly 40 years later - although in my naughtier moments I sometimes do - but I have seen and experienced some great and wonderful things because of Magic. Who could ask for more?

So the techniques do work. Your life can be enhanced. The effort alone will bring wisdom

Alan Richardson
Wessex, England
2006

Chapter One
Magic and Symbols

When I was a youth I borrowed A.E. Waite's Book of Ceremonial Magic *from the library and walked home in something of a daze. It might have been a portion of the True Cross I held. All the tales about such books came back to me. I thought about the members of the Scottish clan Stewart who would wear magically protective bands of iron around their foreheads before they dared to even open the mysterious tome called the* Red Book of Appin. *When I finally got Waite's book home the glamour of the signs, seals and sigils almost sent me into a trance. I spent hours copying them on to paper or using them in various circumstances hoping for a wondrous effect. I am still waiting, however. It took a while for me to realize that they did nothing but exercise my draughtsmanship. But all the same, I was sure that soon I would find some truly magical symbols which would provide the results I wanted, such as opening doors at a touch, projecting me off into the astral plane, and making me irresistible to women. None of which ever occurred.*

Of course I was bemused and befuddled by too much indiscriminate reading on occultism and my own innocence. My gullibility was matched only by that of the writers whose books I had believed in implicitly, both parties believing that certain secret glyphs possessed untold power.

Much later it became clear that symbols have absolutely no power in themselves. Drawings of magical images or electric circuits have no intrinsic power, but by applying the principles they schematise, remarkable results can be obtained. The pentacles which I had so fruitlessly copied

became useful only after I had understood their purpose.
They must *be understood to have any value. A person trying*
to succeed in magic without understanding the symbolism,
will be as big a failure as a driver who cannot understand
the road signs...

ell... Yes and no. I was 17 when I wrote that. Knew everything. It made sense to *me*, so it must be pure Wisdom with a capital Wuh. But there's something slightly wrong with that metaphor about the road signs, and the driver, that I can't quite put my finger on today. I suppose it's because, looking back, I can see now that the sheer glamour of the symbols in the book worked a real spell on me after all. They got me copying, making an effort, wondering and pondering. They did actually exercise far more than my draughtsmanship. So it's not *always* wise to be entirely logical about such matters, though we have to find that out as we go along.

What is Magic?

Everything hangs on this term 'Magic.' First of all, it is nothing to do with giving individuals incredible powers, any more than that the sole purpose of life is the accumulation of money. So far no one has surpassed the definition of magic as 'the art of causing changes to occur in consciousness,' but we usually approach the field in such a state of confusion that even such a simple statement makes no sense at all.

The concept of ritual magic tends to evoke two reactions. The first is one of intense glamour and romance, even though you might not be sure what the topic involves. The second is sheer disbelief and a vague sense of embarrassment. What you might do here, however, is try to see that everyone practises Magic in one way or another.

The first kind of disbeliever is one who has firm religious beliefs of his own and regards anything else as an aberration.

Yet a Catholic, for example, in going to Mass, experiences an act of pure ceremonial magic which might be interpreted by the outsider as having cannibalistic overtones, but yet which invariably has a profound emotional impact within the participant. A change has occurred in his consciousness. He feels a little better for it, and closer to God.

The other kind of disbeliever is one who is a rationalist, non-religious, and who is assured that ritual magic plays no part in *his* life. But unless he is the type of person who has never fallen in love even in the slightest degree, he would be very wrong indeed. The act of falling in love is a ceremony of magic in itself, capable of effecting the most far-reaching changes in consciousness of all. The lover has only to smile or cock an eyebrow and depths within the beloved tremble. The couple share little rites and acts and secret words which are nonsense to the outsider but charged with meaning to the lovers. Simple gestures come to have devastating effect. Carved initials on a tree trunk becomes a living, growing talisman of love. Whatever the outcome of the affair its very existence does something to broaden the psyche of the besotted. Magic at its highest. Changes occurring in consciousness.

The magical techniques given in this book are best seen as ways toward self-discovery, self-perfection or self-mastery if you like. The ultimate aim of a magician must be the same as that of any priest or priestess: Wholeness. Whether the disciplines produce side-effects in the psychic fields is very much secondary to whether they help make one into a better and wiser person. If that disappoints you, then stop now.

It must be admitted, though, that most people come to Magic with some vaguely defined but very strong urge to gain power. I was certainly no exception. Most of us live rather dull lives and exist as dissatisfied and often rather pathetic people. Magic seems to offer a means of by-passing the usual routes to earthly power, and, with a few symbols and a minimum of effort, hints at infinite possibility. In reality, however, while the infinite possibility is most definitely there, the idea of minimum effort could not be further from the truth. Sometimes, being a magician can be the most wearisome task of all. Sometimes, you just want to tell all the Powers in the universe to fuck off and leave you alone.

A true magician is doing no less than aiming for the Ultimate (however he defines that). Metaphorically speaking, Magic is a means of turning inside, grabbing yourself by the scruff of the neck, and hauling yourself up to whatever standards you choose to aspire.

We did it all when we were children, in fact. A child evolves and matures into adulthood by copying the grownups, learning from watching them, and by simulating an adult world by means of play. He adapts to the world by reproducing it in his own terms in play, gradually enlarging his concepts until he can dispense with the play-acting of adult situations. In similar ways, a magician evolves toward God-hood (however you think of that) using rituals designed to reproduce the Inner Worlds. Child to adult, and adult to God, is the evolutionary route; although we all tend to get a little stuck along the way to both.

The Meaning of Symbols

Where do symbols fit into all this? Again, look at the world around ...

The gestures of a traffic police officer are based upon a definite system. Each arm movement has a symbolic meaning, which if misunderstood can result in serious trouble. Each letter on this page is a symbol that is used to express ideas and thoughts in visible form. These letters are far more potent than any Egyptian hieroglyphs, simply because you can understand them, and because they have an effect upon your consciousness. The formulae and equations used in science express ideas clearly and simply to the user, but remain incomprehensible to the uninitiated. Symbols are a means of communication, a form of shorthand. Nor is there anything esoteric about their application. Poets use them, the blind and the deaf use them, magicians and children also use symbols to link with actualities around them.

Magic symbols work on common-sense principles. Where a concept or technique goes against your common sense then leave it alone and wait either for further understanding, or different techniques. Never let anyone in this world or the next tell you that you *have* to do something in a certain way. Never trust blindly anyone in this world or the next. Become a living question mark. Challenge everything.

In ritual magic gestures are physical representations of inner actualities. When a magician formulates, for example, the Kabbalistic Cross, he does so because it is necessary, and not for dramatic effect.

The experienced magician operates on levels of consciousness which are somewhat different from ordinary experience. The only way he can describe these is by using symbols common to us which are lower analogues of that which he is describing. Accounts of primitive people meeting advanced technology and attempting to describe modern artefacts will supply a parallel here. Symbols are a link between the known and the unknown, the outer and the inner. You can project them from your consciousness to try and communicate with the inner worlds: the inner contacts will use them to try and make links with you. You have to evolve your own symbol systems, and make them come alive.

The Lesser and Greater Mysteries

This is not to say that occult teachings can *only* be assimilated through metaphor. In Magic there are the Lesser and Greater Mysteries. The former are the basic teachings whose intellectual contents are available to all. The Greater Mysteries can only be understood through experience; they are beyond words. The

best that can be done is to provide symbols that you may use
as lenses to bring into focus your own blurred intimations of
something greater in this world than yourself. That is why it is
useless searching books for any True Secret. It does not exist.
Books and teachers can only give a few inadequate methods to
reach the wisdom that is nowhere else but within.

In one of his books Aleister Crowley lamented that at his
initiation into the Hermetic Order of the Golden Dawn, he
was given no more than a few astrological symbols and trivial
details that he knew already. Yet that is all that any genuine
group can possibly give. This is a hard thing to swallow, as we
all tend to build up encyclopaedic knowledge of rituals and
the qualities of super-consciousness, and are inclined to expect
more (and more advanced) information, rather than less. Yet
what is the value of hoarding occult details if they do not result
in some progression of experience? It is like a young child
building up a collection of love poems and anecdotes about
the beauty of falling in love. He may reach puberty knowing all
the symptoms and effects, but this knowledge crumbles beside
the reality. Similarly, you may, by analysis of the symbolism
connected with say, Hermes, gain a good idea of what that
god is like, but until you actually makes some sort of Hermes
contact you will not really *know*.

In Western Magic, then, you can be given no more and
no less than two basic symbols: the equi-armed Celtic Cross,
and that of the Tree of Life. The rest is up to you, for there
is no dogma, no secret teachings, no mysterious Adepts nor
anything which can help you avoid doing a great deal of work
to expand these from diagrams in a book, out to vast potentials
within your personal universe. Without a solid grasp of these
two, the rest of them are no more than distractions. These are
the electrical circuits which you will learn to energise.

And you must remember that all the images given are
products of your own making. When we talk about gods,
goddesses, angels and archangels, devas, faeries and the rest, we

refer to personifications of abstract qualities, and we are using these figures to give our minds something to grip onto. These personified images are used to enable you to make contact with benign inner intelligences, but their shapes are entirely of your making. Using one of the more traditional Judaeo-Christian magical systems, for example, we might refer to the Archangel Gabriel, and the element of Water; but in doing so you must remember this: water is a physical parallel of certain qualities within your psyche; the figure of Gabriel is a symbol of these same qualities at a certain level of operation. As you will see later there are other symbols that can be used if these Judaeo-Christian elements are no longer sympathetic, but in any case they are of *your* creation. The point cannot be repeated too often.

Concept Association

Students who come to the Kabbalah for the first time will very quickly find different books contradicting each other concerning allocations of symbols to particular Spheres. The truth is, each source is right in so much as they get results, and it is by concept association that you actually achieve them

We have all at one time seen the hero in a film force some villain into submission simply by grabbing his holstered gun, without drawing it. Behind this is the basic psychology of concept association. The villain knows that if the gun is drawn, primed, aimed and fired, a chemical reaction will occur which will have an unpleasant effect. Thus a simple gesture evokes powerful feelings of fear. It also shows that we get out of symbols what we put into them. The unknowing would be unafraid of the gun because he would not associate the gesture with instant death.

A flippant example? Not really. The laws of magic are the laws that govern our evolution. It is your task as a magician to see these laws in operation in every aspect of life, no matter how apparently trivial or ludicrous.

When you come to work on the images of the Tree of Life and the circle-cross you will pour so much of yourself into certain areas that when you choose to release it all you will be able to direct your consciousness along chosen lines and with determined intensity. With experience, for example, intonation of the God-name for the sphere of the Sun, should positively inflame you with the sense of Beauty and Perfect Balance which are the qualities of that sphere as it appears upon the Tree of Life. A real change in consciousness. A real piece of magic.

If you expected powers, occult domination and the rest, this will come as a real disappointment. Yes, it is to be admitted that Magic can give these if the student were to set his sights so pathetically low, but would it not be better in the long run to aim for real wisdom, understanding and insight into life and living?

Again, that paragraph was written a long time ago. What I wrote then was - and is - true, but I certainly didn't live it at the time. I wanted powers, I wanted occult domination. I wanted revenge on that nasty little man with the horrible dog. I was only human. Am still only human! You *can* get power, but there is always a price to pay, as I'll try to explain later. But if nothing else, magic can give a certain sparkle back to modern life. It gives you a chance to find the *numinous* within the most mundane of events. In a dying, woeful planet it can give you back a little romance, and a glimpse of worlds within and beyond this one. For the final time, it is not in any sense escapist. Anyone who has laboured day after day at all the numerous facets of magic, both intellectual and practical, and who has paid the tolls that magic will inevitably demand, and who has, on top of all this, got on with his workaday job and tried to make a good life for his family (no easy matter either) will know that the real escape is to keep one's head down and ignore all thoughts of spiritual possibility. The magical path is lonely and hard and has to walk in parallel with the routine one - which is lonely and hard enough in itself.

In different ways we need magic more than we have ever done. The Swiss psychologist C.G. Jung had a tower of his own design built on the edge of a lake, at Bollingen. There were no modern amenities within this tower, and it was shut off from the modern world, He wanted to keep in touch with his elemental nature and he would go there when he felt the urge to write, commune with himself, or be alone. In old age he would still chop his own firewood, do his own cooking, and have conversations with his pots and pans as he did so. To him it was vital that Western Man re-discover magic. He saw life in terms of myths and rituals and the religious quest. Over and above all the self-styled Adepts and Hierophants, Jung was by far the greatest magician of this century. And he was entirely self-taught, with not the slightest hint of Tibetan Lamas, Space People, or Arabian mystics guiding him from secret sanctuaries c/o Post Office boxes.

And finally, for those people who are attracted by magic but who still have so-called 'rational' objections to the talk of gods and goddesses and clustering angels, we can take comfort from Brodie-Innes' statement which I quote here from memory: "Whether gods and demons really exist or not is beside the point; the important thing is that the universe behaves as though they do." With that statement in mind and with the magical scheme regarded as a paradigm, we can go a long way indeed. In whichever direction we choose.

Chapter Two
The Magical Philosophy

e cannot go far along the path of High Magic without looking at the philosophy of the Tree of Life and the Kabbalah. The latter word is from the Hebrew 'QBL.' This is a verb which means 'to receive'. It is a reference to those esoteric teachings passed on 'from mouth to ear': whispered secrets which no non-initiate must hear. Alternative spellings include 'Qabalah' (which is technically the most accurate but looks ugly) and 'Cabala.' Those few who insist upon spelling it as Quabbalah should be horsewhipped.

The QBL, then, was an esoteric doctrine passed on from initiate to initiate, a mystic lore that was said to be capable of explaining the secrets of the heavens above and the earth beneath. It was supposed to have been transmitted from God, through the angelic orders to Adam, Noah, Moses, David, Solomon, and finally to Rabbi Simeon ben Yohai, who wrote the teachings down during the second century of the Christian Era.

Its main books were the *Sepher Yetzirah*, or 'Book of Creation,' and the *Zohar*, or 'Book of Splendour,' which was written in Spain by Moses de Leon in the 13th Century.

The theoretical Kabbalah contains elements from ancient Egyptian, Babylonian and Greek philosophies, spiced up with the mysticism of Philo and the early Christian Gnostics, with the doctrines of reincarnation, transmigration, and the enduring realities of Good and Evil, Light and Darkness thrown into the mix.

If the theoretical Kabbalah proved irresistible to the mystics, then the practical Kabbalah proved itself a manna to the magicians. And it is that diagram known as the *Otz Chaim*, or Tree of Life, which provided the framework upon which all else was hung. One commentator described it as the 'Mighty and All-embracing glyph of the Universe and the soul of Man.' Surprisingly, despite the bombast, it is exactly that.

Dion Fortune wrote what is still the best book on the topic in *The Mystical Qabalah*, although this is almost matched by Gray's own *Ladder of Lights*, which more than lives up to its subtitle of 'Kabbalah Renovata'.

According to the revelation, all life preceded via a series of emanations beginning from what we might describe as Absolute Nothingness. This was the condition of the universe before Man, before God, before anything. To translate, it means - Ain: *Nothingness*. Ain Soph: *Limitlessness*. Ain Soph Aur: *Limitless Light*. The light analogy is used because light is the most abstract symbol capable of equating. *Ain Soph Aur* is the source from which Everything manifests. Those familiar with the Theosophical writings may know the concept of the "Days and Nights of Brahma." This idea states that at vast periodic intervals, the whole of the manifest universe returns to the source of Nothingness. This is the Unmanifest, the Veils of Negative Existence, or *Ain Soph Aur*.

Try and picture this absolute nothingness becoming denser at a focal point, until Kether, the First Sephirah, or Sphere manifests. Like a brilliantly luminous droplet of water condensing from a cloud of infinite steam. Kether becomes the Limitless Light in Extension.

So... from that Absolute Nothingness came the single point of pure white light known as Kether, which is that state of consciousness that you might crudely (very crudely) describe as God.

It was from this first sphere, or *sephirah*, that the universe began to manifest itself in the numerical sequence shown, so that Kether (1) is at the level of absolute spirit, and Malkuth (10) is the realm of densest matter. It is in Malkuth, the earth-sphere, that we find ourselves. The Tree provides us with a ladder by which we can attempt to climb back up to our Source.

The spheres themselves are clearly arranged on three columns known as Pillars. All the positive, upbuilding energies in the universe are linked with the right-hand column, and all the negative, breaking-down forces placed on the left. In this sense, however, 'negative' was never regarded as evil in itself, any more than it is evil to knock down buildings (or psychological edifices) which are dangerously decayed. It is wrong to associate Good with Positive and Evil with Negative. Being always positive, always saying 'yes,' can create just as much evil within the world as its unbalanced opposite. The balance, then, is represented by the middle pillar.

Within these columns we can resolve the universe for ourselves, if we are uncompromising enough: Yes/No/Maybe, White/Black/Gray. Sometimes, as all magicians know, the best way to deal with the world is to retreat into the basics, and nothing else.

By analysing the spheres, however, we can add some subtleties to the way that these three qualities express themselves.

We can best imagine the Tree as a kind of filing system which is divided into ten compartments, and into which everything - *everything* - can be placed. Our initial problem is simply that of having the exact nature of this system explained to us, because after that it begins to explain itself.

Had there been 26 compartments then this would present no problem at all, for it would be based upon the alphabet. Into the compartment 'L' for example, would go leopards, lemurs, light, locusts and love. While it would be simplicity itself to store such data the exercise would be meaningless on any spiritual level: it is no good looking for love and finding lice, lugworms and loquaciousness. That won't teach us anything. But with the system used by the Tree we can not only store away our own experiences in a particular area - intellectual,

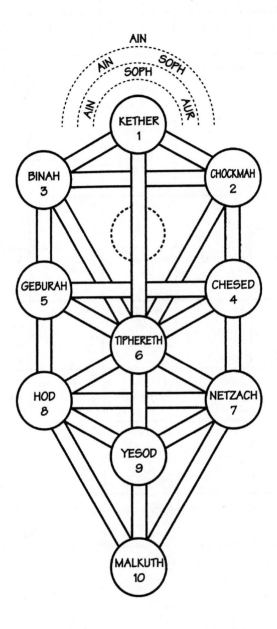

Figure 1. The Tree as a filing system

Sphere	Arch-angel	Divine Name	Colour	Magical Image
Kether	Metatron	Eheieh	Brilliance	Face of an Old Man, in profile
Chockmah	Ratziel	Jehovah	Brilliance	Masculine bearded face full on
Binah	Tzaphkiel	Jehovah Elohim	Black	A mature woman
Chesed	Tsadkiel	El	Blue	A wise king, on his throne
Geborah	Khamael	Elohim Gibor	Red	A warrior king, on his chariot
Tiphereth	Michael	Jehovah Eloah va Daath	Rose Pink	A child, priest-king, sacrificed god.
Netzach	Auriel	JHVH Tzavoos	Emerald	Beautiful naked woman
Hod	Raphael	Elohim Tzavoos	Orange	An Herm-aphrodite
Yesod	Gabriel	Shadai el Chai	Violet	Naked man, very strong
Malkuth	Sandalphon	Adonai	Olive	Mother Nature, on her throne

emotional or spiritual - but we can use to it to lead us on into the collective experience of mankind as a whole.

Each of the spheres upon the Tree has some basic attributions. So do the paths linking them. These are known as the Correspondences. One of Crowley's books was called

Liber 777, and consisted of a series of correspondences for every sphere and path upon the Tree: Magical Images, Names, Letters, Tarot Trumps... he showed where we could place them all, and link one with the other. One of the first things you must learn to do is work out your own Correspondences. But until you've got the confidence to do that, the major and traditional Hebraic correspondences are given in the chart opposite.

And to understand how you can use each of these as keys into areas of consciousness, we need to look at each one in sequence.

Kether

The Crown. The Point within the Circle. Instead of visualising God as some omnipotent deity in human form, visualise him as an all pervasive radiance, underlying all and everything. Then go a stage further and imagine that light concentrating itself into an intense pinpoint which hangs within the absolute nothingness and complete blackness, of the unmanifest universe, before The Beginning. This, then, is Kether: a pinpoint of pure white light which contains All. This is the universe before the Big Bang. This is the Essence.

Chockmah

Wisdom. When Kether became aware of itself it exploded outward in what we might describe as the first Cosmic Laugh. This is Chockmah, which represents the archetypal male and is the sphere of all the outrushing, thrusting and forceful energies as they emerge from the Source. One of its images is that of an upright pole, which should speak for itself in phallic terms. All phallic symbolism, therefore, can find an ultimate placement in this second sphere.

Binah

Understanding. If Chockmah is the sphere of pure and dynamic *force* on archetypal levels, then Binah balances it with the archetype female qualities of pure and receptive *form*. It is the sphere associated with the black-robed Great Mother, the planet Saturn, and that revelation known as Sorrow, in its spiritual sense: 'All life is suffering' as Buddha said, but through that (through Binah) we can begin to understand the deepest parts of life's mystery.

These three spheres are known as the Supernal Triad. They represent the innermost essence of all that we find in denser levels of manifestation. All of us have qualities of positive and negative within us. How we use these qualities, as opposed to over-indulging in them, determines how much Wisdom (Chockmah) or Understanding (Binah) we have. It is nothing to do with what sex a person may be. Men can be Binah figures just as women can relate to Chockmah.

Chesed

Mercy. The planet is Jupiter. It is the sphere of benevolence, generosity, philanthropy, and all those energies which go toward the creation of stable, peaceful civilisations.

Geburah

Justice. Its planet being Mars, it is the natural balance to the sphere of Chesed. It is that energy which ensures that anything effete, corrupt and putrid (however this manifests) is regularly scoured, purified, or swept away completely. Although its traditional symbol is that of the pentagram, the modern image of a surgeon's knife is more indicative.

Tiphereth.

Beauty. Both Chesed and Geburah resolve themselves within Tiphereth, the sphere of the Sun. It is the sphere of all those Sacrificed Gods who abound in major religions, and who bring harmony to the world by dying for our sakes. Harmony is, in fact, one of its titles. Not the placid and often pathetic harmony of, say, an English vicar, but the harmony achieved by the nuclear forces reacting with the Sun itself, with its power to heal or destroy depending upon where we are placed at the time.

This trinity of Chesed/Geburah/Tiphereth is known as the Ethical triad. They represent those qualities which lift us above mere self-absorption toward a consideration of life and humanity as a whole.

Netzach

Victory, or Achievement. This is the sphere of Venus, with all those quickening impulses which might loosely be termed 'romantic,' and find expression in the arts generally and in our emotional behaviour personally.

Hod

Glory, or Splendour. This is the sphere of Mercury, whose qualities of pure intellect neatly balance the raw emotion of Netzach, and which find expression every time we act rationally, and logically, or indulge ourselves in the sciences.

Yesod

Foundation. The place of the Moon, and the unconscious mind, and what we might think of as the instincts upon which so much of our existence depends. It is also the realm of the astral plane, the 'treasure-house of images,' and because of the use made of this by magicians, this particular trinity of Netzach/Hod/Yesod is known as the Magical Triad.

Malkuth

Kingdom. The material world on which we all live and find expression. All of the above spheres "pour down" into it.

Malkuth contains them just as our physical body contains our mind, soul and spirit. It is related to the four elements of Earth, Water, Air and Fire, which we might think of as Solids, Liquids, Gases and Radiations.

There is an eleventh sphere also, known as DAATH, or Knowledge where Malkuth used to be before the 'Fall', but that needn't concern you here.

As you can see from the diagram, the spheres of the Tree are joined by paths, which might be regarded as the blending points. Thus the path between Yesod and Netzach represents that area within our consciousness which rises from pure blind instinct and leads into the glow of more romantic considerations: where having sex turns into making love. Or else we can study that path connecting Hod and Netzach and make the careful balance that we must all strike sometimes between soulless intellect and brainless passion.

So we can begin to see how this unique filing system of the Tree of Life can work. Like a novice secretary, the beginner will handle the system clumsily at first, often putting things into the wrong holes; but with rapidly increasing assurance the peculiar patterns and interrelationships between the spheres will begin to teach of their own accord.

For example, all those gods related to the intellectual 'Hermetic' arts would be equated with the sphere of Hod: Thoth, Hermes, Merlin, etc, while all those figures of romance and enchantment will go into Netzach: Nimue, Nephthys, Freya and so on.

There is no dogma attached to this (or there shouldn't be): militant feminists are quite welcome to reverse the polarities and adapt them to their own peculiar vision of the universe. As long as you make your own attempts to determine the Correspondences for each sphere, that process known as 'Building the Tree in the Aura' will take place. It is when this happens that the filing system starts to become more akin to a super-computer of spiritual possibility.

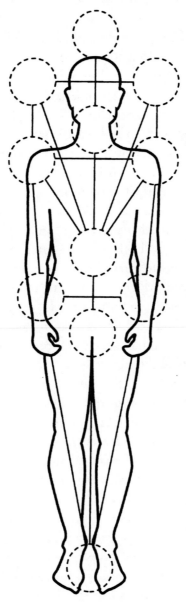

Figure 2 Building the Tree in the Aura

In fact the magicians of the Golden Dawn and all the
offshoots would have done exactly that - building the Tree into
the aura (i.e., fixing it in the unconscious) by visualising it as
shown in Figure 2. They would ritualise it by touching the top
of the head (the crown) and intoning the word *Eheieh*, while
attempting to experience the qualifies of Kether, or the 'pure
white light,' within. Then to the right temple, and the left, and
soon, down the body in the order of manifestation, doing all
of the above while also visualising each sphere in its associated
colour. In time - in a surprisingly short time - the magician
will have a very marked sense of the reality of these spheres.
It is as though the amorphous mass of his psyche has been
moulded into a particular pattern, and highly specific areas
of his consciousness begin to inter-react in the same way as
the spheres upon the Tree. When he comes to work on his
Correspondences (which involves no more than associating
items of experience, symbols, impulses, etc., with the patterns
of the spheres) then he will find links, parallels and suggestions
springing into his mind which will be altogether surprising,
and never less than illuminating.

A magician who feels that he has been unfairly dealt with
might use Kabbalistic magic to seek Justice. He would wear red
clothes, light five red candles, intone the words *Elohim Gibor*
in a fivefold rhythm, and even *think* red, before addressing
his complaint to the Archangel Khamael, visualised as a great,
winged darkly red figure wielding a flaming sword and wearing
a pentagram upon his chest.

This would not, however, be any kind of 'revenge magic'.
Geburah (Mars) cannot be used for that. His plea would be: 'If
these events are right and proper, if it is part of my karma to
suffer this, then so be it. But if it is not, and I am being unfairly
treated then please redress the balance, bring justice back into
my life'.

The actual words are less important than the intention, of
course, but the supplicant should be very strong in his belief

that he is being wronged, for if such suffering *is* part of his karma, or nothing more than his own stupid fault, then the effect of such an invocation is to bring all the energies to a head, sooner than usual, with all the intensified suffering that might ensue. On the other hand, he may well find that balances *are* made in his favour, and ways made smooth, and burdens lifted.

The forces on the Tree are all perfectly balanced with one another. It is impossible to 'trick' these energies into giving something for nothing. There are always prices to be paid, harmonies which will be maintained. And when the Tree is built into the aura it becomes a device which enables us to connect our own limited consciousness with the unlimited consciousness of the universe. Whatever changes we affect within ourselves ultimately affect the whole of existence. We become part of the great cosmic balancing act and must accept a grave responsibility for an inward kind of decency and honesty.

But in purely magical terms it means that in time, the magician will be able to pick up one symbol - an *ankh* for example - and that single glyph will give him access not only to the huge store of his own ideas, but also to the infinite experience of the collective unconscious. By lifting this simple device from the altar of his conscious mind, with ritualistic intent, he is potentially in touch with the experience of every Egyptian worshipper of Isis, every latter-day hippie, every astrologer who has ever marvelled at Venus, and every Roman who has ever adored that goddess as she rose from the sea. It becomes simpler with practise: like driving a car, or handling complex machinery, it becomes almost automatic. In time, you can forget about it all with your conscious mind because it propels you inward from unconscious levels. And then, as so many other magicians have learned to do, you can sit down in some quiet place, summon up your gods, goddesses or guides, and start to perform real magic...

Relating Your Experience to the Tree

So now you have worked briefly through the Tree of Life. Remember that *every* aspect of experience can be categorised into one or more of the Spheres, and you must try to do this with the things in your world. You may see a stern father, for example, spanking a particularly unruly child, and if your immediate impulse in these delicate days is not to get the child taken into care and the father jailed, then you might be inclined to see this as Geburah in action. Later you may see the same man filled with compassion and forgiveness and decide that this is Chesed. And finally, you might glimpse father and son reconciled and happy, and be sure that this is Tiphereth, the Sphere of Harmony, making its presence felt within the pair of them. A doctor, receiving a call on the telephone before driving over to use his skills to heal someone's wounds, is an example of Hod in action, the planet Mercury relating to communication, travel, intellect, and healing of hurts and wounds. A young boy composing a love letter and plotting ways in which he can just happen to bump into his fancy and all the while wrestling with his nascent lusts is an example of Hod, Netzach and Yesod at work. Bearing in mind Binah's title of 'Sorrow' and the name, which means 'Understanding,' we can appreciate that the highest qualities of the latter can arise if we can cope with our suffering and sorrows. While in terms of the dynamic energies of Chockmah, we might ponder Blake's saying: "The roads of excess lead to Wisdom."

A study of astrology here is a great advantage, the character of each planet relating to its Sphere. In practical magic we can use this to our benefit. For example, a ritual dealing with the forces of Geburah would take place on Tuesday (ruled by Mars) at the specific *hour* ruled by Mars. Now whether there really are cosmic forces around at those times which will aid our rituals is not important. By choosing to perform the ritual according to this scheme you are adopting a particular frame of mind from which it will be easier to, so to speak, "take off."

Of course, we can begin to see the Tree of Life now on several levels: macrocosmically it represents the structure of the universe and the forces which shape our lives; microcosmically it represents the inner structure of Man and the qualities of the Self which attempts to assert itself against the Universe. This is just a restatement of 'As above, so below.' Man is a miniature of the universe.

The Importance of Numbers and Colours

Although there is an entire branch of number study known as the *gematria*, it is something that I feel is of only limited importance to the modern magician. On a more simplistic level we can note that each Sphere is numbered in order of descent, so that Chesed is four, and Netzach seven. Thus a square would symbolise Chesed, and a beautiful seven-pointed star Netzach and Venus. Anyone working in the latter Sphere might, perhaps, have seven candles arranged into the star-shape for the same reasons we gave above relating to rituals dealing with martial forces. Further, at the end of a ritual, a magician usually gives ten knocks on the floor. As he does so he visualises the Spheres in order, willing himself to descend in consciousness back to the levels of Malkuth, the tenth Sphere.

Colours also have a place of some importance. Each Sphere has its own particular colour 'frequency,' as we might term it. In the advanced studies on the topic will be found complex and comprehensive charts, but here we need do no more than give a basic outline. We might add at this point also that this is by no means a science. Many popular occultists tend to imply that a certain colour means a certain thing, but too much emphasis on this leads us very close to trivialising the whole topic. So colours for the Spheres as given here should be regarded in the same light as any other symbol.

Malkuth, traditionally, is given the four colours of citrine, olive, russet and black, which hint at the different colours of the Elements as they appear in nature.

Yesod is given the colours of silver-violet, or violet-blue, to capture the peculiar qualities of moon shadows.

Hod is given the colour of orange to express the quality of intellect, while Netzach balances it with green, for this Sphere has connections with the peculiar emotions that beautiful countryside can inspire in us.

Tiphereth is traditionally given the colour of rose-pink, flecked with gold, but this is so much the sphere of the Sun that any brilliant visualisation of this orb will suffice.

Geburah, the martial sphere, is obviously equated with red, while Chesed has the more tranquil colour of a rich blue.

Binah, the sphere of Sorrow, is coloured black, while Chockmah nearest to God is given as iridescence.

Kether itself is beyond mere colour, and is ascribed the quality of utter brilliance.

Thus returning to what we said about the Geburah ritual, we can expand it more and have it take place on a Tuesday, at the hour of Mars, with red as the dominant colour within the colour, and the pentagon as the dominant symbol.

The Names of Power

These, quite understandably, fascinate most people. We are still hooked into the concept that there might, after all, be some magic word which can do everything for us. The Names, like our own names, are no more than keys. If we hear someone calling us, then depending upon who does so, and how they do so, we react inside in different ways. Any teacher knows that the first thing he must do with any class is learn all the names. That is the first step toward gaining any real discipline and (eventually) affectionate response from them. There is a theory that the Names are designed to stimulate the psychic centres (chakras), which seem to have physical correspondences with the endocrine glands, but we will mention this more in a later chapter. More likely their value is that they are, at present, 'none sense' words which we will deliberately fill with the highest concepts we can imagine. Like very private pet names, in fact. When intoned during the working the aim is to tune into the particular energies being invoked and change our consciousness, for the duration of the rite, into that frequency.

Speech as a whole should be adapted to the nature of the Sphere concerned. Normal conversational tones for Malkuth, stern tones for Geburah, and an awestruck whisper for Kether.

So you can see from this that everything can be interrelated and interconnected. Everything must point toward the same idea so that the mind can concentrate its force into definite channels of pin-point intensity. The degree of concentration needed is very great, and naturally there is an early tendency to rush things. But they should be done carefully and slowly, so that the full force of visualisation can be exerted. For it is the visualised images behind the ritual gestures which are important. They give power to the gestures and achieve reality within the Astral Light, which is the same as the unconscious mind.

Expanding Ourselves

But why? Why raise our consciousness to the levels of Chesed? What will happen?

Harking back to the idea that Magic is primarily a means of making us into better, wiser people, then surely any extension of consciousness, any development in experience will serve to broaden our minds. You can take a lesson here from *A Christmas Carol* by Charles Dickens. Scrooge existed for much of his adult life in a state of meanness, bitterness, and downright cruelty. Suddenly, after a most extraordinary extension of consciousness, he found himself able to function in other, beneficent areas. He found himself pushed into therealm of Jupiter, or Chesed, with its largesse, its humanity, and its sense of humour. No one can deny that a change in his consciousness did not make him into a better man. The only difference is that in our case, Magic is a voluntary process.

Chapter Three
The Cross and the Elements

The other main glyph used within the Western Magical Tradition is that of the circle-cross, the Celtic cross, the equi-armed cross of the Elements, to give it various names. It is no more than a circle equally divided by a cross inside it, yet it is as all-encompassing as the Tree of Life itself.

In the Tree, Malkuth is known as the Sphere of the Elements. This, in fact, is our circle-cross. All of the magical operations made possible by the Tree's unique plan necessarily take place within Malkuth. The circle-cross therefore, is your launching-point for ascending the Tree. (The rest of the Spheres fit into this fourfold system rather neatly, but I've saved this for the appendix to avoid clouding the issue here.)

The Circle Cross

In ancient times in Western Europe, where the seasons are clearly defined, a four-point analysis of heavenly patterns was inevitable. The day was clearly seen to consist of dawn, noon, dusk, and night; the year had sharp seasons of spring, summer, autumn and winter; while the constituent qualities of the world were known to consist of Air, Fire, Water and Earth.

The body, for instance, was Earth; the blood was Water; the breath Air; and the bodily heat was Fire.

Nowadays we might refer to these same Elements as solids, liquids, gases, and radiations.

It was (and is) only logical to see that these Elements had parallels on different levels which could be extended indefinitely. In Jung's speculations the four modes could be determined as being Sensations (Earth), Feeling (Water), Thought (Air), and Intuition (Fire). While astrologically the twelve signs are grouped into four triplicities which relate to the Elements, thus:

Fire: Aries, Leo, Sagittarius
Air: Gemini, Libra, Aquarius
Water: Scorpio, Pisces, Cancer
Earth: Taurus, Capricorn, Virgo

You can see within this particular ordering of the Elements a distinct staging process of increasing density from Fire downward. This relates to the so-called 'Four Worlds' of the Kabbalists, which can be categorised as follows:

Fire   Atziluth   Emanation
Air   Briah   Creation
Water   Yetzirah   Formation
Earth   Assiah   Action

You can see this at work in the urge to paint a picture, perhaps. A spark (Emanation) is stuck within the artist's psyche which is nearly imperceptible, Unmanifest Thought, almost. Yet it gradually expands into vague but powerful impulses to paint (Creation) which eventually begin to shape into specific designs (Formation) and are brought to fruition after much physical effort (Action).

So this shows that the Elements can also be used to refer to the most subtle and intangible aspects of our thoughts. They refer then, to the four bases of our physical and spiritual worlds. Were we to make a brief list of correspondences so far it would look like this:

Fire/Radiations/Summer/Leo/Wand/Emanation
Air/Gases/Spring/Aquarius/Sword/Creation
Water/Liquids/Autumn/Scorpio/Cup/Formation
Earth/Solids/Winter/Taurus/Shield/Action

The list can obviously be extended infinitely, and in a later chapter we will add a few more attributions, but there is sufficient there to show that the actual physical elements are worthless in themselves. The important thing is that when you stand at one of the quarters of the magic circle there will be a vast range of concepts in your mind relating to that quarter, giving it an impact within you.

When Bill Gray was submitting his work for admission into the very potent and very influential magical group known as the Fraternity of the Inner Light, as founded by Dion Fortune, he included this chart

Move On And Stop	East	South	West	North
Breathe In And Out	Inhale	Hold	Exhale	Exclude
Call Name	Ooooay	Eeeooo	Hoooah	Hayeeee
See The	Sunrise	Noon	Sunset	Midnight
Think Of Moon At	New	Full	Old	Dark
Feel The	Spring	Summer	Autumn	Winter
Greet Archangel	Raphael	Mikaal	Gabriel	Auriel
Experience The Element	Air	Fire	Water	Earth
Feel	Pure	Radiant	Flowing	Fertile
Feel As If	Flying	Burning	Swimming	Walking
Take And Use The	Sword	Rod	Cup	Shield
Emote	Sorrow	Excitement	Joy	Contentment
Use Magnetism To	Repel	Control	Attract	Hold

Decide To	Will	Work	Want	Wait
Have	Perception	Power	Purpose	Patience
Dedicate	Mind	Spirit	Soul	Body

In many ways the chart given above contains the very essence of Magic. You really don't need much more than this. All of it springs from that simple and universal design of the equi-armed cross within a circle. As I wrote in the first edition:

> *The design of the circle-cross is a mandala, a symbol of the psyche in perfect equilibrium. It is what we aspire toward when we come to practice magic. A person who is essentially 'airy' for example, should make more efforts to bring out of himself more of the other Elements. His aim, after all, is to become Whole.*

Well, I thought it was true then, and even now I can't exactly say that it ain't. I certainly went to great lengths to do exactly what I advised, but today I am still largely a man of Earth and Water, with only occasional forays into those characteristics known as Fiery or Airy. I am what I am, I suppose, though it does no harm and certainly a bit of good if you do try to fulfil the original advice.

The design is also the basis of most group ritual - that is, workings along inner lines with other sympathetic people. But we can leave a discussion of that for another chapter.

Four God-Forms

Traditional magic uses the images of four archangelic figures placed at the Quarters of the circle-cross: they are Raphael, Michael, Gabriel, and Auriel. These are often, for convenience, known as 'god-forms', and you shouldn't get hung-up on whether such beings are actual gods or something less than that. Again for those people (like myself today) who might feel uncomfortable with such Judaeo-Christian figures, be assured that you can easily substitute them with imagery from whatever Tradition is most appealing. Bear with these for the moment, however, so you can see why and how they are used.

There are two main ideas, then, as to what these images actually do. First, there is the idea that by energising these figures (which, remember, are personifications of qualities within our own psyches) with the highest aspects of ourselves, we are, in effect, sending out a signal into the inner worlds. At a certain point this will be answered by evolved and specialised inner entities who can judge by the quality of this signal that they might want to associate with and help us. The images are thus seen as points of contact between this and the otherworld, and are used by the entities as vehicles, for the duration of the working. In a very crude sense it is like advertising one's qualities in a newspaper in the hope of attracting a suitable partner who might share your ideals, although it would not be wise to push that analogy too far.

The second theory holds that these images push through instead into the Collective Unconscious, and that what comes through are selected aspects of the racial group-mind. It is as though we could tap those parts of the genetic structure (if that is the right term) which contain all of man's unconscious inherited learning.

There are many other theories but these are the two main ones. But as to which theory is a more likely explanation as to what these beings really are, is not something you should worry much about. Just get on with it. The traditional archangels of the Quarters, then, are:

Raphael	East	Sword
Michael	South	Wand
Gabriel	West	Cup
Auriel	North	Shield

They are invariably described as follows:

Raphael. Predominantly a yellow-orange figure, young with sharp intelligent eyes, he wears a short Grecian-style tunic for ease of movement (in another guise he is Mercury, god of travel). In his hand is a large sword and emblazoned on his cloak is a caduceus, which you can glimpse as the wind flutters the cloak, for Raphael, god of Air, is a wind-blown figure.

Michael. A figure clad in the colours of Fire, golden-haired, strong, and radiant. He wears a breastplate emblasoned with a lion's head and carries a spear. He is sensed as being a strong, energetic figure, and one who can be as uncompromising as he is helpful.

Gabriel. Clad in long robes of shades of blue and violet. His face is pale with deep-set features. He holds aloft a silver goblet and is surrounded by a sense of Water. His is the type of character one would term "deep."

Auriel. The colours of nature are his, for his Element is the Earth, so his long robes are olive-green, brown, citrine and russet, trailing the ground around him. In his hand is a shield which is understood to represent a portion of the Earth's curvature, while emanating from him is a sense of growth and fertility.

Now although I have used the masculine gender for all of these god-forms it is clear that gods themselves must react with goddesses. So Gabriel and Auriel should ideally be given a sense of feminine qualities. A young and mature woman respectively, perhaps. Or in this feminist age there is no reason why these qualities cannot be ascribed to the two positive Elements of Air and Fire. It is up to you to determine what feels right, regardless of what tradition or your head tells you. For example, those who prefer working with what might be termed the Native British Tradition might prefer: Merlin for Raphael; Arthur for Michael; Niume for Gabriel; Morgana for Auriel.

More of this later, however.

The Magical Weapons

I have mentioned the four Weapons in passing several times. These are the means - the tools - through which the magician can wield and direct energies. Having actual items is not compulsory by any means, but it is necessary to learn about them.

The Sword. Of all the four instruments this is the only one which does not have an obvious natural equivalent, unless it be in the crude form of a piece of jagged flint, or similar. The sword was the weapon which required the furthest leaps of proto-science to achieve. It required a degree of intellect and application that was little short of wondrous. We shall come back to this weapon's significance in a later chapter, but meanwhile we might mention William Gray's speculation that the sword was originally an arrow - an obvious Air attribution. The quality of the sword is that it can cut through obstacles just as surely as reason and logic can cut through many problems.

The Wand. Both a staff which can aid the traveller and an offensive or defensive weapon. Early, natural versions of the wand, or spear, were just fire hardened sticks. They were used also in the control of fire, either as pokers, or as torches in themselves.

We can see here that arrow and spear are but different-sized versions of the same thing. Indeed, were we to view the magical universe in purely dualist terms then it would be one of Black and White, or Fire and Water. In the present scheme, however, Fire and Air are seen to be aspects of the same, positive, dynamic energy. Which brings us to their counterparts:

The Cup. Apart from the associations with the Holy Grail which we will go into later, the cup was originally the cauldron, the communal bowl from which the tribe drew its nourishment and also learned something about being social creatures. The very life of the tribe came forth out of the pot, as the fruit of love came from the womb.

The Pentacle. The shield, or pentacle (or pantacle) was, according to Gray, a piece of material used for scraping the surface of the earth as an early spade, for the planting of seed. This was the tribe's insurance and protection against famine. Again later on, we shall see something of the shield's peculiar link with the concept of sacred stones. Both represent endurance, protections and the Earth itself.

Again you can see that a cup is but a version of the shield folded more into itself - or conversely so. They are complementary energies. As ever, the more you work at it, the greater the number and pressure of the concepts that build up behind a single key image such as the Magical Weapon is intended to be. When a magician takes up his wand (or rod or spear) and holds it aloft in a particular way, it is a signal to his unconscious to unleash the vast hoard of wand-qualities within the magician's psyche.

Some people go on to make actual physical versions of these, but without this preliminary work on the concepts that will 'charge' the Weapons, they will be no more than useless. Others will use the pointed finger for a Rod, the edge of the hand for a Sword, palm of hand for a Shield, and cupped hands for - obviously - a Cup.

Now we can look in some detail at an actual and traditional piece of magical working.

Chapter Four
The Middle Pillar

The basis of this chapter is the exercise of the Middle Pillar. This technique, when analysed, shows the basis of most Kabbalistic magic. Look at Figure 3. This shows the Microcosmic Tree of Life. It is a symbolic representation of the Tree within the human body. What we are specifically concerned with is the Middle Pillar. The Spheres of this pillar coincide with the top of the head (Kether); the throat (Daath); the solar plexus (Tiphereth); the genitals (Yesod); and the feet (Malkuth).

If you are familiar with yogic systems will be aware that these locations bear close relationship to the chakras. More precisely, the chakras relate as follows:

Muladhara Chakra	Malkuth
Swadisthana Chakra	Yesod
Manipura Chakra	Tiphereth
Anahata Chakra	Tiphereth
Visuddhi Chakra	Daath
Ajna Chakra	Daath
Sahasrara Chakra	Kether

The Muladhara Chakra is 'removed' from the base of the spine to beneath the feet, where it is regarded as a storage centre.

The aim of the exercise is to circulate force within the aura, to vitalise it and charge it. Once this is done, the energy can be turned to achieve specific ends which we will deal with in turn.

Look at the charts. What relates to *Kether?* Colours? God-names? Qualities? Selecting these we get:

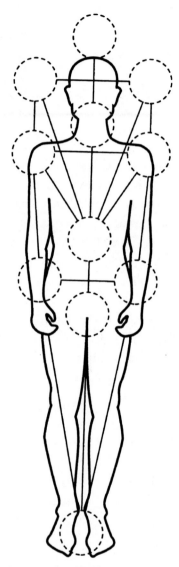

Figure 3. The Microcosmic Man

Colour	Brilliant radiance
God-name	Eheieh (pronounced *Ehy-hey-eh*)
Characteristics	Omnipotence, Omniscience; the Creative Power; Perfection

So, visualise this brilliantly radiant Sphere above your head. Pronounce the God-name rhythmically, and as vibratory as possible. Imagine the Sphere pulsating with the power of the Name; imagine the inside of that Sphere as the universe itself, pounding and throbbing with the Name; and as you say it, bear in mind the qualities of Kether. Remember this is not a glass sphere: it is alive, swirling with energy.

Moving Down the Pillar

Then progress down the Pillar. From the base of Kether shoots a beam of pure energy which flares into the Sphere Daath. The process is again the same, except that the colour is grey, and the God-name Jehovah Elohim (pronounced *Yeh-ho-voh El-Lo-heem*) compounded from the god-names of Geburah and Binah.

Continuing down the Pillar, the correspondences are as follows:

Tiphereth	Solar plexus
God-name	Jehovah Eloah va Daath (Y*eh-hove-vah El-oh vay Daas*)
Colour	Yellow
Yesod	Genitals
God-name	Shaddai el Chai (*Shardi el kee*)
Colour	Violet-blue
Malkuth	Feet
God-name	donai ha Aretz (*Ardonay ha aretz*)
Colour	Olive, russet, black

Obviously you will need to reacquaint yourself with the characteristics of each Sephirah, and also give yourselves new information by searching the charts. This is good, because you will be forced to check and recheck your information until you become thoroughly familiar with it.

To apply the exercise so far, you should be in a room by yourself, lying or sitting relaxed. Hands should be clasped and feet together to complete the circuit.

Circulating Force within the Aura

Now that the chakras are energised, you can turn to the task of circulating force within the aura. This is done by combining breathing techniques with visualisation - the system in yoga known as *pranayama*.

Visualise the egg-shaped aura around your body. Then as you exhale steadily, imagine a brilliant force travelling down the *left* side of the aura, from top to bottom. Hold it there. Now, picture this force flowing up the *right* side from bottom to top, as you inhale. Then repeat this several times. The whole picture should be of a band of force in synchronised circulation with your breathing, flowing down one side into the other, and up again.

Then do the same again, except this time the force flows down the whole front of the aura, and up the whole back. Exhalation takes the energy from the head down over the body to the toes, inhalation sucks the energy back up to the head.

The exercise is completed by the 'fountain' technique. Having completed the preceding steps, exhale strongly and steadily, visualising a column of light shooting up through the body from the feet, and out through the top of the head. The energy travels up the spine, taking the route of the Kundalini. As it comes out it sprays like a fountain, or like the Sahasrara. Chakra as seen by clairvoyants. On inhalation the spray curves down the limits of the aura to the feet again. And so on.

So... you have now energised your psycho-spiritual centres, revitalised the aura, and charged yourself with energy. Or at least you should have done, if you have performed the exercises correctly. And this means building meanings into the God-names, actually trying to *feel* the energy as it flows through the body, and in, out and down through the aura.

As in sport, achievement depends upon constant practice and training. A few half-hearted attempts at this exercise will achieve little. Similarly, training in sports implies more than just a few desultory push-ups.

Gaining New Qualities

This particular exercise can be applied toward practical ends. Sensational writers always promise wondrous effects on the material plane, so we may as well look at the rationale behind this, for there is no doubt that magic *can* be used to gain things on this level. Let us suppose that you have reached a stage in the practice of this exercise when you can really feel the energies flowing and being directed as you choose (and you *will* reach this stage). Let us suppose further that you wish to travel. What you should now do, after completing the Middle Pillar technique is to visualise your aura turning into bright orange, shining with the light of Hod. You would be in the midst of this light, looking out, suffused by the whole glow. As you visualise this you intone the god-name of *Elohim Tzavoos* while identifying yourself strongly with the qualities of Mercury and travel, and communication. You will yourself to believe that all the forces of travel in the universe are achieving a sympathetic vibration with you which will lead to the achievement of your goal.

Having finished this, you then go about daily work, but start to bend your mind to the thoughts of travel and the ways that this might come about. You may find that if when you start applying, you will gain a travel scholarship; or you may find a sympathetic relative; or a sum of money may come your way to enable your wish to fulfil itself. If worked on strongly enough and often the aim will manifest itself through ordinary channels, yet with definite impulses from inner levels. But more than this, you will achieve your effect by putting yourself into a frame of mind which is actively attuned to the possibilities and the half-chance. You will open your eyes and your will to areas in your life that you may not have noticed before, and make efforts along these lines.

Alternatively, you may use the same sphere for a job in, say teaching. In this case you would formulate your image of the type of job and proceed in the same way. What you would *not* do the next day, however, is sit back and wait for an offer to appear miraculously through the letter-box. Like any mortal being you will still have to supply the Malkuth qualities by writing applications, looking at the lists of vacancies, and keeping your ears open for any forthcoming posts. When you does finally get the sort of job you want it may well be because at the interview you were so attuned to the teacher qualities of Hod and Mercury that you were the obvious choice ahead of the other candidates.

I can speak of the above from personal experience. Technically I had no chance in the interview for my first ever job in teaching, but because of all the work I did as described above, I was offered the post ahead of other candidates who were far better qualified and experienced. In fact, it was the start of the worst year of my life!

Obviously, what this technique enables is for the user to evoke chosen qualities within himself. In less complex ways we can do this by singing songs when we feel inspired, or by dancing, or by countless other means. This exercise, however, consciously aims at evoking certain areas, and with specific intensity. You can use it to make yourself feel courageous and strong by using Geburah; or to make yourself feel more harmonious through Tiphereth. Yet these qualities are to be regarded as there already, and the exercise as a means of bringing them out and developing them. It is not a question of courage, or whatever, being grafted on from an outside source.

In his excellent essay *The Art of True Healing* (from which this technique is unashamedly stolen), Israel Regardie goes into some detail regarding the practical application of the

Middle Pillar exercise. Those interested should refer themselves accordingly. In all the attempts to gain material benefit through magical means, however, we must bear in mind the old maxim that what we ask for is very often not what we want. Or to quote from W.E. Butler: "Be very careful what you ask for in magic, because you might be unlucky - and get it." It is like the person who desires nothing more than to be rich, and who finds, on achieving his desire, that it is at the cost of family, friendship, and health. If we are to ask for anything at all in magic it should be in the realm of higher qualities, rather than tangible things, for if there is any one law in this universe it seems to be that there is a price to pay for everything.

Chapter Five
The Banishing and
Invoking Ritual

This is everyone's favourite. Very easy to do. Generations of wannabe magicians have started their very first ritual magic with this one. The very glamorous concept of a 'banishing ritual' is no more than an attempt to create, as far as possible, a sterile spiritual atmosphere in and around the operator. It is no more than what a surgeon would do. The magician's aim is to try and simulate the condition of *Ain Soph Aur* within the place of working. A definite sphere of force is created around the magician in performing this, and even the least psychic of people can feel a real difference in the atmosphere. What we will briefly analyse here is the classic 'Banishing Ritual of the Pentagram'.

This was a devised within the scheme of the Golden Dawn, and is still regarded by many magicians as the standard technique for the particular purpose. But you must remember that it was created well over a century ago. The men and women who devised the Golden Dawn workings were doing so for their own time. Modern versions of the banishing ritual often do without the god-forms and pentacles entirely, using, in one instance, a 3-D version of the circle-cross, and intoning the vowels I.A.O. while using each circle to obliterate Time, Space and Events respectively, from the user's consciousness. Another very senior occultist once told me that if she wanted to purify a room she wouldn't bother with rituals or incenses or smudging or anything like that: she would simply do it, with her mind alone. But not everyone is as good as that, and it's perhaps best to start with something tangible. So while you ought to study this Pentagram Ritual in its classic form for the sake of understanding your magical foundations, do bear in mind that it is rather dated. On the other hand, like the steam engine, it does still work.

The Kabbalistic Cross

The first part of the Ritual is the Kabbalistic Cross. This can be used prior to other rituals than banishing rituals. It is a device for 'switching on.' It symbolises the beginning of the rites, and the user's dedication to the God or Goddess.

Begin by facing east. This can be geographical east, or mystical east, which is simply in front of you, no matter the actual direction. This is where darkness turns Light, presided over by Raphael who associates with Sephirah Hod and ritual magic.

Bring your arms from your sides out and up in a wide sweep and down to a spot just above the forehead (Kether). Your hands should be palms together as in prayer.

This done, say 'To thee God,' then bring your hand down to the solar plexus and say 'Be the Kingdom'; bring them up to the right shoulder, 'and the Power'; across to the left shoulder, 'And the Glory'. Then cross your arms against your body and say 'Unto the Ages of Ages, Amen'. As you do this, visualise a beam of brilliance travelling from above the head down to *the feet*, then completing the cross from right to left shoulder.

In this case, we substitute Tiphereth for Malkuth (the Kingdom), because stooping to touch the Malkuth centre at the feet would make the actual rite clumsy. Thus Tiphereth becomes a symbolic Malkuth for the purpose of grace and ease.

If you study the diagram of the Microcosmic Man you will realise that the Power and Glory refer to Geburah and Chesed (also called Gedulah) situated at the right and left shoulders. So, as the beam comes down, visualise the Divine Force coming to Earth, to link Man with God for the performance of this rite. Similarly, visualise the scourging, purifying force of Geburah cleansing the aura, and the steadying forces of Chesed, balancing these forces, and steadying the aura. Finally, visualise the radiant cross and yourself as gigantic, echoing the words across the universe.

These words in Hebrew are 'Ateh (*Artay*). Malkuth, ve Geburah ve Gedulah, le Olahm. Amen.'

Can you think of any improvements? Any way to make the performance more elegant or effective for you? Try them. They may not feel very satisfactory at first, but they are a step in the right direction.

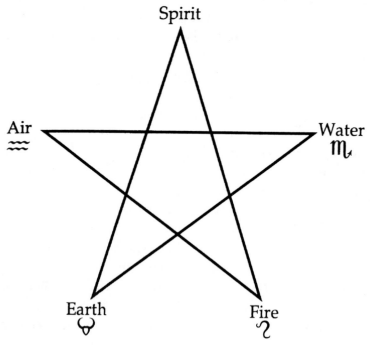

Figure 4. The Five-pointed Star

Tracing a Five-Pointed Star

Still facing east, trace in the air in front of you a large five-pointed star. Start at the bottom left-hand point of the star. Right hand stretched down across your body, bring it up above and in front of you to create the top point, down and to the right to create the bottom right-hand point. Continue so that the other points are about level with your shoulders, and finish where you started. As your hand travels, visualise the star being formed out of glowing energy coming through the tips of your first and second fingers. So now you have a large, symmetrical five-pointed star glowing in the air in front of you, in your imagination. This star is then energised by stabbing the centre and uttering one of the Words of Power. All very glamorous, but what is the significance?

Well, here is one interpretation.

We use the right hand to begin with. We could relate this to Geburah, which rules the shoulder of the Microcosmic Man. Remember we are trying to create a pure atmosphere, and Geburah is the constructively scourging-force to help us do so.

We use the first and second fingers of the right hand, which could be symbolic of rods or spears, which relate to Michael, Fire and Tiphereth, Sphere of balance and harmony.

Also we begin at the point marked Earth on the diagram and trace up to Spirit. Symbolic perhaps that we are transmuting earthly conditions to conditions of pure spirit. And the actual shape of the five-pointed star symbolises Geburah again. Yet there are countless other interpretations. There is nothing profound about this one. Look for your own and the ritual will gain power.

Having energised the centre, turn 90° to your right and do the same again, then twice more until you are facing east again. Now visualise the four great stars surrounding you, glowing, set at the limits of the space available. It can help, when you first do this, by using an appropriately scented joss stick: you

1

can literally see a glowing line being traced in the air, and the smoke holds for long enough to help the imagination, backed up by sensory information.

Building the Archangels

We now begin to build the archangels. Turn back and read about them. Remember that constant visualisation will 'solidify' on astral levels forms which will be ensouled by the corresponding intelligences. These archangels will act as channels for contacting the forces they represent. Being concerned with the creative levels of energy, they also act as mediators of forces which might otherwise be overwhelming.

So, arms outstretched (why?), we visualise Raphael first. Now intone, 'Before me Raphael; behind me Gabriel; on my right hand Michael; on my left hand Auriel. For around me flame the pentagram, and above me shines the six-rayed star.' As the archangels are mentioned, sense the feelings of Air, Water, Fire and Earth. Picture it as vividly as you can. Dwell upon their characteristics as you name them. There is no hurry. Finally finish the ritual by formulating the Kabbalistic Cross again.

At first, all this may seem complicated, but in practice it is much easier than it reads. Of course it would have been simpler for you if the instructions had been tabulated. But in the case of this book, the purpose is not to tell how to do the rituals, but rather why to do them; or at least get you thinking for yourself. That is why the information is not grouped conveniently in one place.

Further Aspects

Now you know how to purify a place in preparation for magical work. There is yet another aspect of this ritual, however, which will shed further light on it. With only one variation the method can be used to invoke particular forces. The variation is simply that you begin the star at the point marked 'Spirit,' and trace down to the Earth point, and so on.

In *banishing*, use the word 'Adonai' as you stab the centre of the star. As you intone the word, picture yourself as a mighty lord cleansing the Quarter you face by power of command and gesture.

In *invoking*, the word is chosen according to the Sphere you are dealing with. Thus operations of Venus would use the God-name of Netzach. As you invoke this force you imagine it coming 'down' and filling you in answer to your calling. Also, the archangels face towards you when invoking, and away when banishing.

So now you know how to banish unwanted forces, invoke wanted forces, and circulate force within your aura. Within the variety of these techniques are the bases for the whole of ritual magic. When you come to create your own rituals, you will use these same methods, even though the application will be different.

The lower triad of the Tree - Hod, Netzach, Yesod - gives us a clue to these techniques. In fact it is sometimes known as the 'magical triangle'. Hod supplies us with the intellectual reasoning behind the rite; Netzach gives it the flair and sympathy; and Yesod links intellect and emotion to subconscious levels so that the concepts take effect as described before. Malkuth meanwhile supplies the physical basis for ritual.

Your Own Name

One valuable technique to use in connection with the Banishing Ritual is to repeat your own name to yourself, seeing the letters, and hearing your voice booming across the universe and echoing back to you. Imagine that the whole of your life-force is in that name. Now cut off the last letter of the name but keep on intoning it within your mind. Now another letter and another, and as each letter is omitted feel your personality fading, feel your whole self dissolving until the final letter of your name is gone and you are just Void and Nothingness. This is another and sonic attempt to achieve some semblance of the quality of *Ain Soph Aur* within. Use it to reinforce and supplement the Banishing Ritual if necessary. The medieval charm based on the word *Abracadabra* is related to this aim. By identifying an illness with the word, then reducing the letters in the word, the illness was supposed to fade accordingly.

Abracadabra

Abracadabr

Abracadab

Abracada

Abracad

Abraca

Abrac

Abra

Abr

Ab

A

And after this I would emphasise the need to return to normal consciousness by a reversal of these techniques. Always always ALWAYS do this.

Chapter Six
Astral Magic

The next technique uses your imagination, without the support of any ritual gestures. Essentially it involves the creation of forms in the Astral light which are used as vehicles for the Inner Intelligences they are aimed at. These forms are sometimes known as 'telesmic images.'

This system of working is generally known as Astral Magic. It belongs to the realm of Yesod, sometimes called 'The Treasure House of Images.'

In some cases, the method involves visualising yourself as a particular character in a symbolic mental drama, the aim being to evoke the qualities and experiences of that character in yourself.

You may well question the validity of this system. The obvious criticism is that the user will be living in a dream fantasy land, a self-induced fairy-tale. This is true of course if the user forgets the correct approach to symbolism - the approach we have stressed throughout the book. But when you are a competent magician, using a controlled symbol-system, you will always be aware that the images are your *own* creation.

Even so, where is the psychology behind this? Where is the contact with everyday life?

In answer, turn back to that earlier definition of Magic as a means of growing up.

Hero Figures

At various stages of your life you will have felt the need for myth and hero figures. These are necessary. They supply us with symbols of aspiration. They show us something of the standards we should try to achieve. In very young children, the hero figures are their parents, whom they copy and identify with in their games. Later, they graduate through traditional folk-heroes to contemporary ones. In each case, the children hope to be able to recreate the experiences and attitudes of these figures within themselves.

Some of these we outgrow, like Santa Claus and Robin Hood; others we continually aspire to, particularly in the fields of religion and sport.

This is why the family is so important. If the parents supply the appropriate hero qualities, the child will benefit. Unfortunately, this is not always the case. Often, the child has to find his own hero figures. For example, a child lacking in paternal influences may choose a figure expressing manliness and virility. Hopefully he does not choose to copy the local thug.

We outgrow these images when we have absorbed the qualities built into them by our imagination. It is simply a matter of identity-seeking, which is a step on the way to fulfilling the maxim of 'Man - Know Thyself.'

All this is in the realm of Yesod, which among other things is also sometimes known as the plane of illusion. Think back to the times of your first love. Think how that person seemed to be the most perfect creature alive, at first, yet remember how the illusion faded slightly if not completely with time. We build up images around things which either fade with our own increasing maturity, or remain because their qualities are still above our own immediate potential.

Yesod is concerned very much with the formative years of puberty, when the need for myth figures is great. But the lesson of Yesod is one of independence on all planes in all ways. As more and more of the Yesod-ic qualities are absorbed, the dependence on heroic and father-mother figures becomes less and less. It is a process of seeing through the glamour of things which obscures the true essence. Much of the hideous glamour of magic is there because we have put it there ourselves, and one of the purposes of this book is to strip some of this glamour away.

Although this is an apparent digression from Astral Magic, it is important that you understand the everyday psychology behind it.

Background Ideas

Remember it is not the images themselves that are important, but the forces or collective experiences behind them. The mental psychodramas involve archetypal symbols and characters taking part in situations beyond our normal experiences. We try to absorb some of these experiences, or rather, try bring out of ourselves the qualities we are looking for, using carefully chosen symbols which will link with inner actualities.

Changing ideas about the symbols will show up as changes in the symbols themselves. Great concentration is needed, for it is useless to rush through the working. You must take it slowly, examining each step and every symbol, building new concepts into them. As the concepts develop, the symbols will gain in power. At best, you can become aware that your consciousness is functioning in another and very real dimension

Essentially, Astral Magic is meditation materialised to visual imagery. Some find this more palatable than the meditative analysis of abstract concepts, but we must think about this. Many people take to this way of working because the relative austerities of mysticism become dull and boring.

A Working

What follows is the first path-working I ever devised. It seems very odd to me now, and almost laboured in its style and direction, but so many people have written to me telling how effective they felt it was, and how they managed to connect with their 'inners' because of it, that it must have done the trick. So I leave it here....

Sit or lie comfortably, breathing calmly and steadily. Empty your mind of all extraneous thoughts and images. The journey begins from a beach - not an ordinary beach, but one with sand of citrine and olive colours. You are lying on this beach, a few yards from the sea, with the beach itself stretching away behind you to infinity. The sun burns down, but its rays do not tan. Instead they inflame you with a desire to trap the rays at their source and absorb them within the innermost recesses of your being. You reach out to catch them, to touch the sun which seems so huge and near, but you fail and sink back on the sand.

Beneath you feel the earth, firm and solid and massive, with you as a mere speck upon the surface. It offers firm and solid comfort, far more than that distant sun. Even so...

But you are drawn away from these thoughts by the sense of the sea so near to you. Sitting up, you look across its waves of surging violet. Suddenly, the whole surface is disturbed by a mighty figure, a classical Neptune, rising out of the sea. Laughingly he raises a silver cup filled with sparkling liquid, and offers it to you, and then sinks invitingly back into the sea before you can accept. Deeply moved by this awesome, god-like figure, you pace the nine steps down to the surf and wade in, and as you do so, you melt into the sea: you become the sea and feel its currents and tides as your own. For a seeming eternity you stay in that state completely at one with the sea, but gradually, persistently, there comes a beckoning call from above.

The caller is Michael, clad in his robes of fire and pointing at you with his spear. Seeing the kindly wisdom in his eyes, you remember your original urge, and call out to him with all the force of your spiritual yearning.

You re-organise into a compact entity. No longer are you the sea; it is time to reach further. Gripping the butt-end of the spear which is offered to you, you pull yourself up to face

Michael. *Immediately behind him is a colossal sun within easy reach in but a few steps. Michael smiles at the fear and hesitation you show, but taking you gently by the shoulder, he leads you towards that sun. As you get nearer, you realise that it emanates spiritual intensity rather than physical heat, and the rays engulf you, blotting out everything but the swirling golden clouds flecked with rose and salmon colours, which stream and shape into a whirlpool. You cannot see Michael now, but you sense his presence nearby. All you are aware of is being sucked into that vortex, and thrown out on to firm ground again.*

The worst is over, and as you look around, you feel a confidence and inspiration that you have never known before, you feel that you are on the fringe of a known but long-forgotten land. The colours of fire, the flame-shaped mountains in the distance, all conspire to set alight something inside you. But your immediate concern is the road that you are standing on, a broad road leading to a building in the distance, and straddled by a huge golden hexagram. Michael is back by this time, and he gives you a push in the small of your back to set you out towards that place. As you step through the hexagram you feel like a lizard that has lost his old skin - lighter, happier. Close to the building now, you pause at the bottom of the six large and high steps leading up to the doorway...

On either side of the doorway is a lion, growling. But remember that you have come a long way, gone through some strange and new experiences, and to turn back at this stage would be the action of an undedicated coward. Now you walk a sure and steady line between the lions which you find are not as big as they had seemed at a distance, and certainly not as frightening.

The inner chamber now. Six-sided, with an altar in the middle large enough to take a person lying down. And so you do so...

*Now invoke the spirit of whatever sun-contact you want
to make, using whatever system you use, be it Apollo, Horus,
Michael, Arthur, Christ or Whoever. For the purposes of this
working which is essentially Kabbalistic, let us stick with
Michael. Realise that the person who has been leading you
was just an earthly image of you own creation, ensouled by a
partial essence of your own Michael-ic qualities leading you
here. Now that you have raised your consciousness nearer
to that of the Source, invoke Michael himself that he may
enfold some of the Tiphereth qualities within you.*

*Whatever it is that you want to achieve, visualise it; see
yourself in the future as you want to be in relation to the
qualities you are aiming for. Or perhaps you want some
answer to a question that is concerned with the affairs of
Tiphereth. If so, then ask it. Do not expect some booming
voice to answer, however. Rather look for some quiet
realisation in the near future.*

The important thing now is to retrace your steps exactly the way
you came. You have just raised your consciousness somewhat
(how far depends upon experience), and now you must return
to normal levels, so go through the stages of your journey in
reverse, until you end up at the beach again.

Analysing the Working

Today there are vast numbers of books offering endless varieties
of path-workings. It is up to you to use the Virtue of Malkuth,
'Discrimination', to decide which ones are connecting with
sources of genuine potency, and which are merely self-indulgent
short stories.

As stated, there is no reason why the one given above cannot
be adapted to Pagan practice. The hexagram is a universal
symbol of opposites in perfect balance: Fire and Water, Male
and Female, Positive and Negative. It is a symbol of us all as
we cope with the good and bad, the bright and dark, the lucky

and the unlucky aspects within us. Tiphereth is the realm of the Sun, that sphere which holds all things in its orbit, and which itself is comprised of colossal, opposing energies held in perfect balance. Whatever God or Goddess the magician may identify as being central or radiant to his cult, can be used with or without the six-pointed star. Working along these lines, in this direction, means that the magician will be entering areas of individual and collective experience in which the principle of 'Willing Sacrifice' occurs.

In a simple way readers can make a start at contacting the essence behind each of the spheres by asking themselves a series of simple questions:

Malkuth: Have I ever asked why am I here? What am I doing?

Yesod: Have I ever had intense, evocative dreams?

Hod: Have I ever gained satisfaction from using my intellect?

Netzach: Have I ever known moments of great passion and romance?

Tiphereth: Have I ever willingly sacrificed anything for the sake of others (e.g. sacrificing a career for the sake of children)?

Geburah: Have I ever made a stern but absolutely impartial decision on any situation?

Chesed: Have I ever been generous for the sake of being generous?

Binah: Have I ever known great sorrow, which has brought understanding?

Chockmah: Have I ever known a great surging of joy in which all things seemed possible?

Kether: Have I ever known the still, small voice within?

These and other questions can literally be asked of yourself, and those experiences which form the answers remembered as intensely as possible. It is as if certain groupings of brain cells were being explored in sequence, and activated in varying ways at varying levels. The more we can relate every aspect of our own lives to the groupings or Spheres in question, the greater potential we have for illuminating ourselves. Symbols such as the hexagram then become a means of tuning into the energies we seek.

As with everything else, these very simple questions are purely examples. You can and should ask yourself many others. The magical techniques using the visualised journey and specific symbols are integral to this process. They are often means of formulating questions and receiving answers before you become *consciously* aware of having asked. Using them all together, you can create a battering ram which can smash though barriers in the mind.

Although we began in this instance by starting from a beach, many of these workings begin from a temple, the direction of exit being governed by the type of working. Some of the preliminary exercises in magical training involve the creation of an inner temple. It is the astral temple created by a trained imagination which is most important, rather than the physical, outer temple. It is the astral equivalents of the magical weapons which actually give them their force, linked as they are with the subconscious mind. The principle is quite readily found in lovers' keepsakes: to anyone else they may be items of junk, but to the lovers concerned they are treasures indeed, which can retain a curious power of enchantment for the rest of one's life. It is the memories, associations, and subconscious links which thus give the items their power. This is why you must visualise the temple or weapons or whatever, embodying the concepts you want. Take modern advertisements which read something like: 'How to be a real man, and prove irresistible to women!' In most cases the secret is in imagining yourself as a smooth, suave charmer and repeating that well-known phrase which suggests: 'Hour by hour, day by day, I'm more attractive in every way.' The ideas here are much the same, being aimed at bringing out certain qualities by means of the controlled imagination.

Visualising a Temple

So you can now begin to visualise a temple, building it piece by piece, and setting it firmly in the astral levels of your mind. Let it be in whatever outward shape which appeals to you - a castle, a cottage, or something in the Grecian style - but it is wiser in the early stages to keep it as simple as possible. Inside it should be a four-walled affair to correspond with the Elements. It is going to be the starting point for the magical workings, so the floor tiles might be coloured according to the scheme of Malkuth. The walls might possibly be hung with tapestries depicting the Man, Lion, Bull and Eagle of Aquarius, Leo, Taurus and Scorpio. The altar could be a double cube of black and white upon which lie the magical weapons, covered by a silk cloth.

These are the general details; the rest you must imagine for yourself, for it is you who will be working in it, no one else. Visualise the scene strongly and regularly, beginning from here with your Astral Magic, leaving by a hidden door behind the appropriate tapestry and returning by the same.

Over a period of time you will come to alter the shape and style of this astral temple as you would a real house. Eventually it will fix itself firmly within your mind. Perhaps you might think of it in terms of Jung's tower at Bollingen. Here is a place you can go when you want to shut out the mundane and trivial and attempt to commune with your deepest self. You must especially learn to visualise the approach and entrance-way to this temple. The opening of this door should be a deliberate signal to shrug off the last vestiges of the petty and the mundane, and leave outside anything which is inconsistent with the concept of this as a temple.

At one level what you are doing is creating at least one place within your world where everything is peaceful, secure, and

devoid of the crassness of the outer world. This is why time
and concern should be devoted to building up this image. It is
after all a temple, an holy place and sanctuary, where you can
find the qualities of spiritual stimulus, warmth, nourishment,
and security.

Aleister Crowley, in his trek across China, realised that due
to the relative nature of Time and Space, he could actually
bring his temple in Scotland to him, so to speak. Of course he
meant the astral equivalent of the physical temple, in which
he could perform just as effectively. When we talk about
something being on the astral plane, however, we are simply
saying that it is in the unconscious mind. So the inner temple
- no matter how simple - is all that we need to work from, even
if it is at present impossible to set aside an actual room for the
purpose.

While on these lines, here is another example of visualising
which may be useful.

Begin in your temple, standing next to the altar facing east.
Now imagine yourself growing, quickly and steadily, growing
far above the temple which is at your feet somewhere below,
seeing the curvature of the earth become a full circle as the
whole globe beneath you. See the stars coming closer as you
grow ever bigger, see the earth disappear completely, feel
yourself absorb suns, planets and galaxies, until there is nothing
else to absorb and you stand supreme as the Heavenly Man
himself. What do you feel now? What are the implications of
this? What practical purpose could this exercise have?

These questions you have to answer for yourself, as no two
persons' reactions are the same.

Of course there is no reason at all why you should not
combine these techniques with some of the ritual methods or
Middle Pillar exercises, and your own ingenuity will tell you
how.

The Magical Personality

We mentioned earlier the use and value of hero figures and god-forms, and detailed the characteristics of the four major Elemental figures. What you must consider now is the creation of your own magical personality.

It is obvious that while we contain the whole of the Tree within ourselves, nevertheless by virtue of our individuality we tend to gravitate toward one Sphere, or one Element. In the early stages of study efforts must be made to gain an understanding - a *connection* - with all the Spheres, but there comes a point when the mature student will inevitably, almost imperceptibly, find himself specialising in one particular area.

Something of this is hinted in the 'Grades' within magic, from Neophyte up to Ipsissimus, taking in all the varieties of Adeptship on the way. Nowadays the idea of vertical progress is very much outmoded, and rightly so, but it does give us the idea that we can cleave to a particular Sphere. Thus in the old system an Adeptus Major would be a specialist in the Sphere of Geburah; that is, his psyche is such that it purely expresses the uncompromising qualities of Justice, Severity, and Courage. On the other hand, someone else may tend to exemplify and channel the qualities of Venus. But the latter is in no wise inferior in spiritual status. Thus a Priest of the Moon is every bit as potent as a Priest of Jupiter, but in differing ways.

It is an obvious point, perhaps, but one well worth emphasising.

What you must eventually determine is your precise area of specialisation. Usually it will be quite obvious: after all, to be reading so far in a book on Magic in the first place indicates at least some self-awareness. But whether it is obvious or not, the following is a useful exercise.

Magic Mirror

This involves no more than examining yourself in the light of each Sphere and determining how you measure up. Get a good book on astrology and see how each planet functions and malfunctions within yourself. Supplement this with detailed readings on the Spheres of the Kabbalah itself. Brutal honesty is required. There is no earthly use in trying to glamorise yourself to yourself. It can be a salutatory experience to see just how lacking you are in areas you had not even dreamt of before. It can be rather like having some utterly disinterested authority figure giving us a long and blistering list of our faults.

After this, regular returns to this 'magic mirror' can help reinforce your attempts to progress toward greater wholeness, and prevent complacency. It is also a means of combating the peculiar smugness that is inherent in many occultists, who seem to associate the concept of 'spirituality' with superiority. Perhaps that is why in Dion Fortune's group each initiate had to take the oath: 'I desire to Know, in order to Serve'.

However, assuming that you have built some secure foundations and are quite certain of your own Sphere, what must you do now?

You must conceive of the very highest qualities of Selfhood to which you would aspire. Again, there ought to be nothing petty within this conception, nothing banal. You must determine the type of person you will to be, and in your meditations try to *feel* some of these qualities; you ought to create internal scenes whereby you manifest these qualities in various fields of action.

This is the first step, but one which will carry on over an entire lifetime as your insight and aspirations expand.

The second step is to create the vehicle which will contain this vast cloud of concepts.

This is, in Magic, the rather nice term 'Body of Light,' which generally refers to the astral body but which we can adapt to mean the self-image of the magician operating at his deepest levels of consciousness.

You must then must determine which Sphere is most akin to yourself. In most cases one of the Paths would be more appropriate, but in the early days the relatively clear-cut Spheres are easier to use. Let us assume then, that you chose the Sphere of Yesod.

Somehow, from the mass of lunar symbolism, a design must be chosen. Imagine yourself in silver-violet robes, perhaps, adorned with lunar images, a head-band with a crescent symbol set on your brow, and with a cowl. If you are unhappy with your everyday physical shape then you can alter it in your imagination into what you deem appropriate. When in your imagination you are adorned thus, you exemplify all of the highest qualities of the Moon you have been studying and sensing for years. The assumption of this image (or god-form, if you like) is the signal to assume those greater-than-normal qualities. You become a Priest or Priestess of the Moon indeed, functioning more closely towards your true Self. But only for the duration of the rite.

In time, when you have some surer visualisation of the images, you may come to make your own robes to match these inner ones, but these are still early stages. Not everyone feels comfortable wearing actual robes, even if they fully understand the psychology behind them.

Magical Names

I mentioned earlier the use and value of the 'Names of Power' connected with each Sphere. One of the first things you must do as a magician is to create your own Magical Name which will sum up the qualities toward which you aspire. In the first stages of study you can simply use the god-name of a Sphere, but when shades and subtleties become apparent to the inward gaze, you have to find some Name to summarise them. It is common knowledge that the pen name of the English occultist

Dion Fortune was derived from her motto "Deo non Fortuna"; W.B. Yeats' Magical Name (or Motto) was "Demon est Deus Inversus," or D.E.D.I. as he would sign himself; Aleister Crowley began as "Perdurabo" ('I Will Endure unto the End') and developed to 'To Mega Therion,' the Great Beast.

Now your own Name doesn't need to be in Latin, Greek, or anything else beyond your ken. It doesn't have to take the form of mottoes, either. Any invented word which somehow sums up what you feel expresses your highest Self will do. What is important is that you do not publicise the Name; that you tell no one - no matter how close they are. It is to become your one secret, your ultimate Mystery. It will express who you are. When the Name is found it will provide one of the most important of all the keys to invoking and controlling very great levels of energy indeed. You should spend time throwing together combinations of words and syllables even though the early results will inevitably sound weak or even downright silly. However, as is the way with magic, the right name for the moment will eventually assert itself. It will feel right. It may change over the years but so do we all. It is up to us to initiate the process.

Switching Off

So now you have a whole range of techniques whereby you can slip out of your mundane consciousness and key yourself into a Magical Personality that can project you into new realms of experience. You must always be careful however, to make deliberate efforts to 'switch off' when the workings are over. This shifting of gear is a common enough occurrence in everyday life. The man who dominates his subordinates at work and yet who is submissive at home is simply exercising different aspects of his nature. There should be situations in all of our lives whereby we can use several gears, otherwise we would end up straining the engines. Ritual and the Magical Personality provide the extra gear and the broad road to be able to cruise with ease at high speeds for a while.

Chapter Seven
The Tarot and the Tree of Life

One of the most important aspects of the Western Magical Tradition is the Tarot deck, and its relationship to the paths on the Tree of Life. The origins of the pack are unimportant. Whether they are from Ancient Egypt or medieval Europe does not matter. The fact is that they provide us with a wealth of profound imagery which we can use to push even further inward.

The deck itself is split into two portions: the Major Arcana, consisting of 22 cards, and the Minor Arcana, consisting of 56 cards divided into four suits which parallel those of the playing cards we know today.

Now whether by accident or design the 22 cards of the Major Arcana seem tailor-made for the 22 paths on the Tree, but it is here that generations of students have become ensnared by attempts to find the 'true' system of attribution. However, it should be apparent by now that there is no such thing. The images of the Tarot are there for you to interpret for yourself and thus gain a measure of real affinity with them. Likewise, it is a test of your own perception for you to be able to place the cards upon the Tree according to your own understanding of both. It is quite irrelevant that Crowley or Waite or Fortune might have written something about a particular card if you yourself suspect a completely different interpretation. Adhere to your own analysis - but keep an open mind.

There are of course many varieties of Tarot decks. Perhaps too many. Some would have been better off saving a few trees by never being published at all. But a few others, such as the *Robin Wood Tarot* by Chesca Potter and Mark Ryan, the *Wild Spirit Tarot* by Poppy Palin, and the awesome *Thoth Tarot* by

Aleister Crowley are excellent. But for our present purposes we will use the images of the Waite/Rider version.

A.E. Waite, even taking into account the era in which he wrote, must rank as one of the most excruciatingly boring and obfuscated of all the occult writers. Yet somehow, in collaboration with Pamela Colman Smith, he has presented us with a truly extraordinary symbol-system for use in the Kabbalistic scheme.

The deck on its own, though, is rather like having a road map in thick fog which will only become useful when some landmarks can be found to enable us to orient ourselves. The landmarks in this case being the Spheres on the Tree. So this is the value in making the effort to align the cards with the various paths: it will give a very definite sense of direction and new impetus.

The paths, as we might imagine, are important in themselves. Crudely put, they are the areas in which the qualities of the Spheres meet and mingle. Thus the path between Yesod and Netzach is, very basically, that area within our psyche where instincts and emotions are blended. This in itself of course says nothing, which is why a visual symbol at this point becomes of enormous value in helping us to focus.

Fortunately no two students agree as to which of the major cards ought to fit on which path; or if they do agree on this then they disagree on the interpretation. Which is right and proper. There should be no dogma within the magical tradition.

In the past century the most usual way to attribute the cards had been simply to equate the first card with the first path and so on down the ladder, pushing the card known as The Fool in at the end. Or else The Fool, zero, would be related to the first path and the Major Arcana would follow on from that. Undoubtedly these methods have yielded some valuable information but, I feel, they have limited themselves by feeling obliged to retain the numerical sequence of the deck.

Of all the differing arrangements the one that seems most reasonable is that given by William G. Gray in his brilliant book *Magical Ritual Methods.*

As we can see from Figure 4, the deck appears to fall naturally into terms of positive, negative and neutral, as does the Tree itself. Starting with the Middle Pillar we note a progression from Malkuth to Kether by way of Moon, Sun, and Star. If nothing else, these cards actually relate to the spheres concerned, which they do not in many of the other systems. Interestingly enough, the progression of religious worship often takes just such a path: from the lunar and matriarchal systems of the Celts, for example, changing gradually to the solar and patriarchal systems as Christianity was introduced; leading to the intense and purely individual stellar consciousness within ourselves. Or perhaps to some stellar religion which may be forthcoming in the Aquarian Age.

On the left-hand or negative pillar we can see cards like The Devil, Death, The Hanged Man, and The Tower, while the positive side of the Tree contains The Empress, Temperance, Strength, The Emperor - all essentially beneficent and secure images.

The three horizontal paths equate with different levels of fate, or free-will: The Wheel of Fortune being pure random chance events arising from the qualities of reason or romance and the whims of both; Justice which is more purely karma, and which connects with our ethical sense as well; and Judgement which is our own assessment of our life in the light of mature wisdom and understanding - such as is said to occur as part of the after-death experience.

At the very bottom of the Tree you can see The World and The Fool, symbolic of unindividuated humanity of differing types, while just above them are symbols of figures we have been talking about throughout this book: The Magician and The High Priestess. They are both linked with Yesod, and remember that it is through connection with the unconscious that Magic works. In the former we have the purely Hermetic type, while in the latter we have the Orphic. Even a cursory glance at the High Priestess with its symbols of sea, moon, and sexuality shows it to be an especially relevant attribution.

But not, in any sense, the *correct* one. Only you can find that.

With The Lovers we can see something of the mechanics of love, and it is a wonder why, with the huge solar image of Michael above them, no one has sought fit to put this card in this position before. While opposite, in The Chariot, is the sort of person whose intellect is such that he develops an acute insight into the world at large even though he himself rarely goes out into it, and is fastened into one place as the charioteer of this card is fastened into a cubic stone. The Philosopher's Stone, perhaps.

The image of the lightning-struck Tower connecting Tiphereth and Geburah is obvious, while we can see both solar and jovian symbols within the card known as Strength.

The Hanged Man and Temperance at the supernal levels on the Tree show different ways toward wisdom and understanding, while at the very top The Hermit and The Hierophant show different ways to express these qualities for the benefit of those souls struggling up after them.

It is impossible to go into any depth about individual cards and paths here; but just to show, however, how well the Waite Tarot deck fits into the scheme, have a brief look at just one of the cards and its path.

The Hermit

This is the ninth card of the Major Arcana. It features a tall patriarch in robes of dark gray or black, standing on a mountain top. His face is in profile, he holds a lantern in his right hand and a staff in his left. In the distance are other snow-covered peaks.

Now in Gray's system of attributions this card is placed on the path between Kether and Binah. We might note that he shares the same colours as the latter Sphere, and is a creature of Silence, which is also one of the titles of Binah. His face is remarkably like the Magical Image of Kether - a bearded king, seen in profile - while the mountain-top symbolism reminds us that we are indeed dealing with consciousness at supernal levels. Taking the hermit's staff as the centre-line, if we equate this with the Middle Pillar, then we can see that the lantern is being held at the Binah position. You might decide that he is looking down at struggling humanity and lighting the way for them. Unlike his counterpart The Hierophant or Master Magician, he leads by example rather than by precept.

At this point you should also apply a similar approach to the position of The Hierophant and determine how the two complement and balance each other, working down the whole Tree in the same way. Ignore the usual divinatory meanings given to each card and simply regard each image as a new piece of art to be interpreted in the light of certain principles. In the early efforts it may seem that very little of original value is forthcoming, but as the student gets increasingly familiar with both Tarot and Tree it will come to feel as though a dam is beginning to burst.

In this way each card will begin to come alive within the psyche, broadening the limits of awareness. This is all that is meant when occultists talk about imprinting the Tarot or the Tree within the aura. It is not, as might be imagined, a case of magicians going about as though they had fairy-lights within their auras, festooned like Christmas trees; it just means that these arcane glyphs have rooted into the unconscious simply because their user has worked hard at putting them there. You can see again the lower Spheres in action within this process: Malkuth, the physical process involved in the student sitting down with pen and paper to analyze the glyphs; Netzach, the desire and imagination providing the impulse. Meanwhile, Hod provides all the intellectual processes needed for interpretation, while Yesod is the bowl of the unconscious - the powerhouse- which will store all the data for future use.

Tarot Magic

When you get tired from this considerable effort you can choose an exotic diversion to get you over the dry patch. This involves one of the visualisation techniques whereby a Tarot card is imagined as a living scene into which it is possible to step. You might find yourself inside the card of The Chariot. You will talk to the charioteer and ask him why he is embedded in stone, what is the significance of the black and white sphinxes, and of the canopy above him. Even if there is no apparent result or else nothing more than a fanciful response from your own imagination, it is still a means of becoming so thoroughly acquainted with the images that you become like best friends, gradually giving and receiving thoughts that could never come from strangers.

For example, begin with the Tarot card The Moon. After all the preliminary clearing and tuning techniques have been done and the astral temple created, find yourself looking into the scene of that card, determined to explore that path which leads from Malkuth to Yesod.

In your Body of Light find yourself facing the pylon gate in a twilight land, with wild beasts howling at either side. What, you ask yourself, is taking place behind those square windows high up in each tower? What is the significance of the tears that the lunar orb seems to be shedding? What will you find at the end of this rough road when you get beyond the distant peaks? You must then visualize yourself as actually walking along this path, keeping a lookout for the denizens of the world around. Images will arise. Nonsensical ones perhaps, but interesting nonetheless. When you finally crest the peaks depicted in this card you will see, perhaps, a Moon Temple, surrounded by nine maidens and Mysteries taking place within. The task is then to seek admittance to this place (Yesod) and see what else you may learn.

At the end, no matter how little you may feel that you have achieved, you must retrace your steps until you end up back in your own little astral temple and ready to step back into Malkuth again.

It is an interesting technique and one which can yield surprising results in time, but it must be emphasized that it is, by and large, a diversion. The real work can only be done through mental sweat and conscious study of each card. No matter how splendid the visions that may arise during any astral magical exercises, unless the student can relate these to fundamental concepts and experiences within his mundane world then he will find them of no earthly use. Inducing visions is easy. The hard thing is to induce wisdom.

Divination

Using the cards for this purpose is an excellent way to learn more about them. The important thing in this process is not in being able to predict the future but in learning how the cards can relate to each other, and modify each other.

Most students are advised to use the famed 'Ancient Celtic Method' of divination which is given with virtually every deck. In truth the method is neither particularly ancient nor especially Celtic. It is not even very clear.

Also, it is extraordinarily hard to do a divination for yourself. For other people - particularly unhappy people with a real and pressing need for some glimpses of the road ahead - the Tarot deck can come alive, as any reader will know. The messages behind the glyphs will spring out almost unbidden. For yourself, in a similar state, the spread often does no more than give expression to your gravest, most pessimistic fears.

Magically, while we may occasionally be able to foresee forthcoming events with surprising clarity and accuracy, there comes a point when we actually create that future which lies much further ahead. That is, we do not so much glimpse it as make it happen. This is Magic in its highest sense.

You should actually begin with a spread for yourself, though, no matter how difficult this may be to interpret. After shuffling the deck and cutting it in whatever manner seems appropriate, with either hand, place the first ten cards in the positions of the Spheres, starting with Malkuth and working upward.

This, you must realize, offers a pictorial representation of your character and psyche *at this moment* of time. By analyzing each card in the light of each Sphere, you undergo a very real kind of psychoanalysis. This may be appallingly difficult at first, if you are still in the stage of 'Gee, who *am* I?' but it gets easier (and often more unpleasant) as you get to know yourself more. Don't approach the deck in the hope of flattery.

The Spheres can be crudely categorized as:

10. Environment.
9. Instinctual drives and dreams.
8. Mental life and/or occupation.
7. Emotional life.
6. That which is central to the querent's life.
5. That which will come to affect it. Karmic balances.
4. Home and security.
3. Greatest worries.
2. Greatest hopes.
1. What the querent can hope for.

It is like the Rorschach ink-blot test. What do *you* see? If, say, The Hanged Man appears in the Sphere of Venus, what possible message can this hold? In what way can this be symbolic of your love life? Are you being turned upside-down because of some great passion, perhaps? Or if there is no great passion in your life at all, perhaps you need to overturn a possible selfish and unattractive personality in order to develop the radiance and insight that might attract a mate? You have to ignore the instruction booklets. Decide for yourself, always.

No one should get too manic about this kind of self-analysis however. Working at it hard and consistently and with exquisite self honesty is one thing. Becoming obsessional is another.

As stated, when you do a spread for yourself the cards will often say the very last things you might want to hear. But as a new-born magician you must never be afraid to challenge them, and thus challenge Fate itself. This is one of the classic ways to wisdom, after all.

You could actually identify your ideal spread and deliberately place the cards in the pattern of the Tree, putting whichever you would most want to appear in the appropriate Sphere. The spread which then presents itself before you represents the person you most want to be. Calling up your god-figure again you can affirm: "In the name of (N) this is what I will to be," while visualizing these images in your aura. In time, with effort and will, you will grow into them. By then, you will have decided that the next phase of personal growth will use some completely different images.

A fast, very simple method of using the cards is to cut the deck first thing in the morning and ask of it: 'Show me a card which might symbolise the day ahead.' At the end of the day, after analysing the events in light of that single card, you can then ask 'Now show me the card which will symbolize the lessons I have to learn from today.' Speak to the deck out loud. Treat it as a conscious entity. Play games with It.

Another very simple technique is to choose one card to represent yourself, often known as the Significator. Usually you would choose from one of the Court Cards: a King or Queen for an older person, a Knight or Page/Princess for someone younger. However there is nothing wrong with a little bit of arrogance, once in a while, so it might be easier to choose something from the Major Arcana.

While holding the Significator, then, and brooding over a particular problem which is causing you concern, you can shuffle the deck, insert the Significator, and shuffle it again.

In a sense, you are sending the card out like a detective whose job it is to track down the true source of your worries. All you do then is simply cut the pack and see what card appears. This, you will understand, will hold a symbolic answer to the question.

Using the cards in conjunction with the Tree is like an astrologer determining what effect a planet will have in any given House. However there is no standard method for Kabbalistic divination. Nor should there be for any method of divination. It is all a matter of how the individual relates to the energies within, using symbols that provide a direct route to the subconscious mind. There is nothing easy about it, no way of avoiding hard work.

Quite simply, magical understanding is like the starlight in The Hermit's lantern. If you want it, there is a long, lonely and bitter climb to reach it, and there are no shortcuts. Remember that the long correspondence tables of organisations like The Order of the Golden Dawn and the rest were composed by ordinary people as capable of erratic thinking, and filled to the brim with as many personal quirks and idiosyncrasies as the rest of us.

You must never be in awe of self-styled adepts and spiritual teachers. If they demand awe from you, then they are not worth bothering with. As regards the use of the Kabbalah and the practical methods of application, there is actually so much magical lumber lying around these days that we can do no better than make a clean sweep at the very beginning of things. Return to *Ain Soph Aur*. Get back to Nothingness. Start with the very basic images of the Tree and circle-cross and build up from there. Say to yourself: "I am what I am - and my magic will be a reflection of this."

It is not easy, but it is the best way of all.

Chapter Eight
Mythological Magic

In an age when so many people are desperate to find their roots and validate themselves either by tracking back their genealogy or else by chasing after their past lives, it is vital that we get back to our spiritual sources. Much, if not all, of Jung's work showed how important it was for every man to have his own myth and to live it out. In the same way we must come to do the same with the ancient images of those mythologies which strike the greatest chords within. It is hardly surprising that people are beginning to do just that, for as Jung said "Everything old is a sign of something coming." The current renaissance of myth and myth-based fantasy, such as deluges the bookstands these days, is a sign of the changing consciousness of our times.

In Magic, as we have seen, many of the major images or archetypes are drawn from the Judaeo-Christian tradition which dominates our Western heritage. Yet the fact is that to young minds the idea of archangels and the like is not especially sympathetic and is even quite embarrassing - even when that person understands the purely symbolic nature of such. Now although there are sound psychological reasons why we ought not to ignore these old images (and indeed why we *ought* to begin our training with them) we might at some point consider the use of images from more appealing sources closer home. As a young man scrutinizing A.E. Waite's ponderous text, I could not have imagined using anything other than Judaeo-Christian imagery. As I move with reasonable grace through middle age, I relish my Paganism.

Every race and country has its own mythology, of course, which is often linked to the 'spirit of place' and the actual soil. The mythologies and spiritual practices of the Native Americans, for example, were not so very far removed from what was practised in pre-Druidic times in Western Europe, but modified by landscape and climate. Just as the history of a nation can be described in terms of successive invasions by different peoples, over long periods of time, so can the mythologies of each be regarded as akin to rock strata. Some magicians, then, are quite happy with the Judaeo-Christian surface on which they stand, in the dust of which they inscribe their Circles of Art. Others are constantly impelled to dig deeper. Yet all the levels support, nourish, or give drainage to the others, if the truth were known. The Pagan, Wiccan heritage is in no way inferior to the Christian, and vice-versa. While at the end of the day, or the beginning of the aeon, it will be the new upsurge of the Native American tradition which will provide the generations to come with the soaring heights they will need; while the religious and mythological topsoil of the present, will sink down to become the bedrock of the future.

Americans, in fact, are in a unique position. As shown in my book *Earth God Rising,* ancient impulses figure just as much in the national life of the New World as they ever did in the witch-haunted lands of the Old. Presidents Lincoln and Kennedy, for instance, provide clear modern parallels to the Pagan exemplars of the Divine King and Sacrificed God. And even numinous, charismatic figures from the world of rock music and the movies can be seen as manifestations of inner energies relevant to us all. In Europe these energies are often summoned and stirred from the remote past and brought forward into the present by various occult groups of both Pagan and Christian inclinations. In America similar energies sparkle in the present and have the potential for opening up the future. If this seems paradoxical at first, then it will become clear the moment that the individual makes links with such imagery.

That which occurred over thousands of years in Europe and elsewhere, often comes to the boil within a few generations in America. There is an old Celtic myth about the bubbling cauldron of the Goddess, which can give a person all knowledge if he can just drink from it. America, the melting pot, can be regarded by its inhabitants as just such a cauldron. It is up to the individual to stand on tiptoes and peer over the brim, into the bubbling contents, and use the ladies of choice and whim to scoop out whatever seems most nourishing.

There is no reason, therefore, why a modern American may not work the magic of Egypt or Greece, or of the Native American tradition. There is no reason why he or she may not work with Merlin or Odin, or Quetzalcoatl. These mythological or magico-religious systems are all levels of consciousness, laid one atop the other, though not one of them is in any way spiritually superior to the others. In personal terms, as an Englishman of Celtic background and tone, pledged to the Horned God, I have occasionally felt compelled to work with the Egyptian pantheons also - and there is not one drop of Egyptian blood within me.

The only question that American readers need ask themselves about the systems of other nations is, do they appeal? Do they strike any chords within the heart? And the fact is that while neophytes may fool themselves into thinking that they are studying old mythology in order to awaken near-forgotten gods, it is really these same gods who are studying *them* in order to awaken their potentials.

Again, as an Englishman, I should only write about what I know best, and have experienced. So if I am to give any example of how we may apply the Tree of Life to some apparently unstructured systems, then the best example I can give is that of the Arthurian cultus.

Several important writers have dealt with this elsewhere, in different ways, notably Christine Hartley in her *Western Mystery Tradition*, and Gareth Knight in his *Secret Tradition in*

Arthurian Legend. Both of them insist that the tales within the Arthurian Cycle contain fragments of occult lore of incredible age, and that Arthur, Morgan le Fay and the rest were hereditary, initiatic titles rather than specific historical personages.

In many ways the Arthurian images offer the best of both worlds: Christians and Pagans alike can find whatever they need within that tradition. I know many Christian magicians who resonate to the energies of Merlin; and no member of Wicca could possibly wish for a better contact than Morgan le Fay. The actual central figure of Arthur Pendragon was hailed throughout England, Scotland and Wales, among the Celts and the Anglo-Saxons; he was venerated all over Western Europe also, as far afield as Italy and Germany. In a strange but very potent way his cultus also staked a very important claim before that gate to the Otherworld known as Hollywood.

It is a major topic, and clearly there is no space here to go into much detail - especially about some of the Celtic equivalents - but I hope to throw out enough to excite the reader into his own researches.

Arthur and Tiphereth

Arthur is central to the whole scheme. Without him it falls apart. He is a solar figure par excellence. Consider the three Magical Images of Tiphereth (see Figure 5):

Child: Arthur was born of an illicit (and magically arranged) union between Uther Pendragon and Igraine. The babe Arthur was spirited away by Merlin to be raised in the Forest Sauvage. The tales of his coming into this world depict him as a true Wonderchild.

Priest-King: Arthur was always more than just another regent. He was credited with amazing deeds of a spiritual nature. His court was more than a court and something of a holy assembly instead. Christine Hartley opines that 'Arthur' was in fact an initiatic title handed down through the ages.

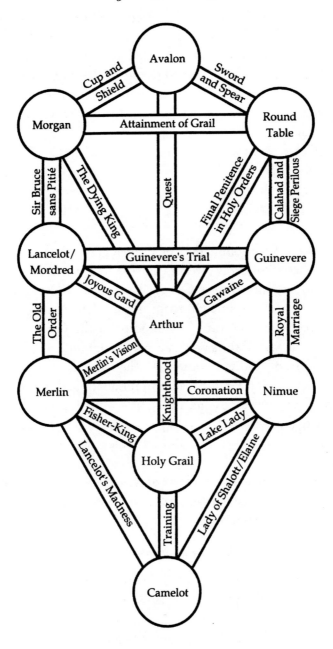

Figure 5

Sacrificed God: After the last battle Arthur is seen to have sacrificed himself for his country. Yet like all Sacrificed or Solar Gods he does not die but is carried away to Avalon, resting until he is needed, when he will rise again. The parallel between this and the Christ image is obvious. Researchers have also pointed to the connections between Arthur, St. George, and St. Michael.

In Celtic terms we can see similar qualities in Cu Chulainn, Eochaid Airem and Tuan MacCairill; and also with Taliesin and Llew Llaw Gyffes.

The Holy Grail - Yesod

This is the very foundation of Camelot and Arthur's reign. It is what transforms Arthur and his knights from a mere body of chivalry into a Goodly Company whose questing was in more than purely physical realms. The Grail gave the Arthurian epic its power. The concept of the Grail as a cup fits in well with Yesod's symbolism as a container and receiver and means of storing impressions. The symbols of cup, water, unconscious, and Grail are all profoundly linked. Thus Yesod is the powerhouse - the unconscious - which contains all our instinctual drives; and the Holy Grail's arrival at Camelot on Pentecost was what gave the Round Table its impetus, its *raison d'etre*.

The cauldron myths are close equivalents in the Celtic realms of course, and notable examples are in those cauldrons or pots owned by Keridwen, Dagda, Bran, Matholwych and Pryderi.

Camelot and Malkuth

This is the Western ideal of the perfect world, a gleaming, pleasant and secure place. Not heaven, but an earthly equivalent, an accurate model. It is the sense of what we aspire to build in our own lives. The Irish parallel of the Four Holy Cities (Finias, Falias, Gorias and Murias) with the four Treasures (or Magical Weapons) forms a neat attribution to this Sphere too.

Merlin and Hod

An obvious equation given Hod's link with the Hermetic Path. Merlin and Hod are both 'initiators' in the sense that they begin things. It was Merlin's magic which enabled Uther to sleep with Igraine in the first place, while he is linked with both the Sword in the Stone and Excalibur. He was the guide and mentor of Arthur, a role which typifies Mercury's nature. He is omnipresent throughout the West though often with other names, such as Lailoken in the Celtic lands and Scottish borders. He is closely linked to the smith-gods which are so important in all European myths, so we can see parallels with Creidne, Govannon, as well as with more magical types such as Gwydion, Diancecht, Manawyddan and Mongan too, although that figure is more appropriate to the path connecting Hod and Tiphereth.

Netzach and Nimue

Nimue or Vivienne, the young enchantress, the otherworldly creature of irresistible charm, a true Venus-figure. Merlin could not resist her, and no man can. She is seen as Fand, Doon Buidhe, Blodeuwedd (the 'flower lady') and in negative aspect as the young Irish goddess Flidias, with her insatiable lust.

Guinevere and Chesed

This is the sphere of stability and expansion and increase; the task of every king being to find himself a queen and ensure this. Without one the monarchy would be incomplete. In the earlier French versions Guinevere was far from being the silly feckless woman who ruined Camelot, but a force in her own right - learned, witty, humane, and popular. A fine equivalent is the goddess Bridget, or Bride, the hearth-goddess, while comparable figures include Etain, Grainne, and Olwen.

Lancelot/Mordred and Geburah

Both of them in different ways managed to bring about
Camelot's destruction, Mordred by design and Lancelot by
the result of his love for the queen. They are alter egos to
some extent. In some versions, however, it is Mordred who
is Guinevere's lover and whose dark figure hearkens back to
the Irish Mider, and earlier still to the Greek myths of the
Underworld. Other figures include Diarmaid and Kulhwch.

Morgan le Fay and Binah

Here we come to the Triple Goddess symbolism of the third
Sphere, common to most mythologies. In this case we have the
three sisters Morgana, Morgause, and Elaine. Sources differ as
to which of the two former slept with Arthur, their half-brother,
but for our present purposes Morgana is the better choice. She
is the Queen Witch and her name means, 'sea-born' - reference
to the 'Bitter Sea' which is one of the esoteric titles of Binah.
Thus in giving birth to Mordred, from her womb came the
forces which eventually brought the breakdown of the cycle.
She is directly equated with the Irish Morrigane, and her two
sisters Babd and Macha, while Keridwen also is a major figure
for Binah, as with Don and Danu.

The Round Table and Chockmah

A single figure at this point could fit conveniently (such as
Galahad and Perceval, both Grail-winners) but better still is
the astrological image of the circle of the zodiac itself, which
is the traditional 'mundane chakra' for Chockmah. Not a
single planet, understand, but the complete wheel of collective
experience which totals Wisdom. The obvious parallel is that of
the Round Table, a body of perfect men directed to the highest
aspirations and balanced around a single point in harmony and
equality. In Ireland we might consider, collectively, the gods of
light known as the Tuatha de Danann, or Finn MacCumhail's

'Red Branch Knights', or else individual figures such as Dagda (connected with Morrigane), Lugh, the High God, or even Cu Chulainn again because of his peculiar dynamic nature, and whose whole death fastened to a single standing stone reeks of Chockmah symbolism at a certain level.

Avalon and Kether

This is the heaven-point, where Camelot transcends toward the concept of the Holy Realm of Logres and its blissful otherworld of Avalon. Equivalents are to be seen in Annwn, and also in Tir na'n Og. However we must remember that Kether, however we analogise it, is always the highest concept to which we can possibly aspire. Avalon represents one possible attribution, but perhaps the best one is still that of God himself.

Now these are meant as guidelines only, for it is obvious that in the Celtic areas particularly, each image is open to much dispute. One advantage of these is that we have an immediate sympathy with them. We can use them just as well as the traditional correspondences as long as we can think of them as more than human figures. Whatever the demerits of the old archangelic images they at least have the advantage of being, for most of us, blank and clear forms without any suggestions of taint. We must therefore try not to think of Arthur as just some dirty but tough old Romano-British warrior who lived in the sixth century, but a veritable Sun-god of native traditions. Let us, then, look at a very simple rite which might help us get them fixed in such an attitude.

Invocation

After all the preliminary work has been done, the magician faces east. Instead of Raphael however, this time he visualises Merlin, according to his own conception of that Mage. He says: '*Before me Merlin...*' The figure in this case is not wielding the sword but offering it to the magician. He remembers how Merlin is connected with the magical swords in the Arthurian cycle, and feels the breeze flowing against, indeed cutting through him. He feels the qualities of life, vitality, sharp intellect, and zestful questioning.

Turning to the south he acknowledges Arthur in the same way, instead of the sun-god Michael. He sees him with his spear or lance (called in Wales 'Ron') and feels the qualities of light, strength, courage, authority and intuition flowing into waves of heat.

The west next, and the beautiful young Nimue. He sees her as through a pool. She carries the bejewelled and wondrous scabbard which had such potent healing powers, and the magician feels a sense of depth and tides, ebb and flow, and the qualities of love, passion, delight and rapture.

The north now and Morgana in starlight, holding the shield which was given to Galahad, emblazoned with a cross of ever-fresh blood, and the sense of slow growth and seasons, crops and plants around her, expressing the qualities of learning (in the experiential rather than the academic sense), endurance, maturity, tolerance.

Facing back to the east again he visualises these figures around him then actually begins to walk slowly around the circle, clockwise, at each Quarter pausing to assume the role of that god-form and attempting to project the appropriate qualities. He circles inward, spiralling slowly to the centre.

At the end of the rite, facing east once more, he turns to each Quarter and takes a slow breath, as he does so visualising himself as absorbing each god-image, willing each one to take root within himself - willing himself to become a more complete person through these.

Again, we can tune ourselves into each sphere by some more simple contemplation, which can be adapted according to the sexes:

1. You know Avalon if you have ever felt any kind of 'heavenly homesickness' and an urge to return to the Source.
2. You understand the Round Table if you have ever felt

uplifted by membership of a close and harmonious group or family.

3. You have felt Morgan if you have ever known the dark and brooding powers of Woman.

4. You know Guinevere if you have ever turned a house into a home, or loved two people equally at the same time.

5. If you have ever been drawn to the edge of madness by loving too much, or if you've ever fought for love, then you know Lancelot.

6. If you have held a family or a workplace or a classroom together, and often suffered for it, then you know Arthur.

7. If you can recall the delights of infatuation, or wept in movies, then Nimue is not too far away.

8. The moment you practice magic, however simple, you become Merlin.

9. If you have dreamed of something greater than yourself, which could transform you, then you've glimpsed the Holy Grail.

10. If you have ever had an ideal of a perfect place to live, then Camelot beckons.

These are hardly high-powered philosophical questions, and they relate to only very simple aspects of the spheres concerned, but they do serve to show how we can make myths relate to our own experience.

Arthurian Tarot

Obviously there is as much scope for this as for the foregoing. We can all design our own Tarot, but it does not necessarily have to take on a visual form. We do not actually have to draw the images. Again the scheme given on the paths here is meant as no more than a device to whet your appetite. There is not the space to go into detail but we could begin, for example, by comparing the Waite card The Emperor with the tales of Galahad and the Siege Perilous; or The Tower with Lancelot's castle of Joyous Gard where he eloped with

Guinevere (previously called, incidentally, Castle Dolorous); or The Magician with the lame Fisher-King; or The Hanged Man with Arthur's death and his transport in the barge to Avalon in company with the Three Queens.

So what you must do now is find out as much as he can about whatever mythology most appeals to your nature. The more you learn, and the more you play around with the images by means of such master-glyphs as the Tree of Life or circle-cross, the more energy becomes available for making your magic come alive. At the same time you can adapt every aspect of your daily life to this purpose. The more you study mythology, even of the simplest kind, the more you will become aware that your own life is not that far removed from the great impulses symbolised by the most ancient tales.

Chapter Nine
Group Work and the Individual

hen we hear about ritual magic for the first time we inevitably conjure up visions of robed men and women in a circle. In a ritual based upon the circle-cross design, for example, the 'officers' of the Quarters try to project the appropriate qualities to create the psychic interplay and balance of the forces of life, within a miniature cosmos of their own. This is rather like a gyroscope which depends upon the perfect balance of all its parts to stay in a constant position in regard to all else. Indeed, the gyroscope even looks like an expanded version of the circle-cross, and in a group ritual involving four people, each representing one of the Quarters, the same cyclic balance can be achieved. Eventually, though, the ideal is that you become the centre or axis of your own cosmos rather than the outer periphery.

Well, that's the theory. And at its best it really does work like that, which can make the lone practitioner can often feel that he or she is missing something profound. But in reality, human nature being what it is, everyone falls out with everyone else when it comes to group work. To a certain extent that is inevitable: belonging to a group, lodge or coven enables the individual to evolve to such a point that he either wants to hive off and create a group of his own; or he achieves enough stability to prefer the solitary path and avoid all the power games that inevitably arise among highly individual souls.

But, assuming all is going well, how can group work can be so potent?

We all know the great joy that derives from occasional gatherings with our nearest and dearest. There is a peculiar and very definite group-mind created which can cause simultaneous impulses within the whole group. Despite the diversity of characters there is nevertheless a remarkable sense of unity, and we learn from this. Qualities from others tend to rub off on us. It tends to provide a sense of deep well-being.

In group-work the aim is to create just such a harmonious unit, but one whose effects are likely to be even more far-reaching as the aim is toward Inner levels of amity. The efficacy of ritual work in groups is not because there is more power as such, but more harmony, more Wholeness.

The simple rituals given in earlier chapters can easily be worked with others. Instead of one person visualising the god-forms of the Quarters, they can be represented by actual people, each one in harmony with his Element. They would be likely to meet seasonally, and thus align themselves with the earth's own sweep around the sun, and all its changes therein. They will align themselves with the natural harmony of things at magical levels and find balance within a chaotic world. In the earliest stages a good beginning might be for companions to jointly practice the exercises of Tarot path-working, the whole group taking a journey through The Moon with one person directing out loud and asking the others in turn what they can see. A definite unity of response can result from this. The operators can be simply sitting next to each other with eyes closed and holding hands. Very simple. Very effective. What happens is that the moment you start to do magical work, you send out a signal on the inner planes. If the work is steady and determined and thus produces a strong signal, then it will soon be answered, and often in the most surprising ways. In due course people of similar affinities will be drawn into the orbit of the magician in question. The possibility of forming a group will arise.

The important thing is not *what* techniques are being used, but in the fact that you are actually doing *something*, regularly and with determination. The inner contacts, which are the true sources of magical energy, are not concerned with how naive or downright silly a person's first attempts at magic are, but in whether they are doing anything at all, with dedication and some attempt at originality. Besides, the word 'silly' originally meant 'holy.' So there is no room in magic for those who might sneer at the early rituals and exercises of others.

Even so, the fact remains that some souls do seem fated never to be allowed access to any group, through no fault of their own. That was the case with myself. By the time that membership of such became available to me, I was no longer interested, and quite happy to continue on my own, with all the difficulties and the many freedoms that this entails.

Each person does in fact 'belong.' No matter how isolated they may be in physical and geographical terms, apparently consigned (or condemned) to a lifetime of solitary magic, they are actually part of one corporate whole. They are members of an inner group (tribe, clan, call it what you will) which exists partly in this world and partly in the next. Therefore, not all of the members are incarnate. And the earthly ones do not need to be connected in spatial terms.

The members of my own small 'clan,' for example, have gathered over many years. They are scattered over the world. We have never met en masse and never shall. Some of them have no overt interest in magic at all. Yet I know that each one is there, somehow, and part of me, and always has been, and that our individual work and consciousness in some strange way always gels.

It's no secret that for a long time I seemed to be overshadowed by the shade of Dion Fortune, which caused me or helped me write the very first biography of that enigmatic woman - which has been plundered, and sometimes quite ruthlessly, by many others since. I am by no means the only person who has felt her inner contact though. Although she has long since gone from my psyche she did seem to be behind a very short summation of my own magical ideas which I called 'The

Microcosmic Doctrine' as a cack-handed tribute to the real source, and Dion's own classic work 'The Cosmic Doctrine', which is as unfathomable to me now as it was nearly 40 years ago. The words below are my own, but the presence behind the words, the impulse and energy, came from what I chose to think of as Dion Fortune herself:

> *All magic is essentially tribal. This tribe can best be visualised as a circle (or even a sphere). Half of it is in the otherworld, half in the earthworld. It is a circle which links past, present and future and makes no distinction. The tribe contains souls which are incarnate, souls between lives, souls which have ceased incarnation, plus beings which have never been and never will be incarnate.*
>
> *Each tribe has a succession of leaders in the earthworld. Their job is to bring through the Magical Current. In their turn they are overshadowed by tribal leaders from the otherworld - what are termed the 'Secret Chiefs.' In fact, if we can, think of that as being in the sense 'Chief of the Clan McDonald,' or 'Chief of the Clan McGregor.' The tone and the style of the tribe alters according to which Chief and which earthworld priest or priestess is predominant at the time. The tribe might grow, change, or contract, but the centre will remain the same.*
>
> *When a newcomer links with the tribe he can tap the collective wisdom of the tribal mind. Often when this happens he has visions of what may appear to be past lives but which are more nearly tribal visions, or points of collective experience down through the ages. These are not always to be taken personally.*
>
> *Sometimes the newcomer will feel him/herself overshadowed by a tribal member from the otherworld. A mistake can be made here by believing him/herself to be an actual incarnation of that entity.*
>
> *Tribes can, do, and should overlap. The Chiefs and the earthworld leaders come and go, but their essence remains*

within the tribe. The Chiefs, therefore, are not meant to be worshipped, for they are points of contact between the worlds. They are part of us as we are part of them. Each member of the tribe is part of one corporate whole. We cannot worship them for we would be worshipping ourselves.

Whatever intellectual output might result is less important than the personal sense of contact with the otherworld, and linkage with the collective consciousness of the tribe.

I give this simply to offer the consoling message: we are never alone. The only danger to the student of magic is if he jumps into it too soon via the numerous commercial cults that exist. There is no denying the appeal of these. I personally wasted endless time and money on them, although even that was a test of my powers of discernment and discrimination. There can be few Lamas, Galactic Magi and Great Masters who do not have my name on their mailing lists from years ago. The *real* magical groups are formed by those people who have gravitated toward each other and feel sufficient empathy to wish to share on deeper levels. As indicated, it is no more than a matter of very good friends who may or may not have shared previous lives together, and who may or may not have some spiritual potency, gathering together as would anyone else. To put the commercial groups into context, let us assume the reader has a group of people whose company he particularly enjoys, such as old school friends; or it might be a single person like a best friend or spouse. The companionship here is of paramount value in his life. He would not dream, therefore, of advertising in a magazine for other people to share this deep harmony, much less offer to teach it for a monthly fee.

Too often we are swayed by the claims of the self-styled Adepts. Claims which are made with incredible sincerity. In each case we hear ourselves asking: 'He sounds like he means it. Why should he lie? He *must* be speaking the truth. Why should he lie?'

For power, adulation, wealth, an enraptured following, wealth... In this material world the question ought to be: Why *shouldn't* he?

Before they get smug, occultists are the most innocent of people in this respect. People do lie, of course they do. Or else they take drugs, or fool themselves. What often seems to occur is that the budding Great Master has a visionary experience of some sort. What he does, however, is credit the vision with intrinsic and external reality, and thus he becomes taken in by something which is only symbolic of unconscious elements within his psyche, a kind of junk mail promising the earth. Visions occur in Yesod, remember, the Moon and Sphere of Illusion, the crude levels of which are broached by psychedelic drugs or a raw natural psychism. This may well be why some of these cult figures are so very sincere about the most absurd teachings, because they really have seen *something*. On top of that, with a following of excitable and credulous people, the group-mind is enough to give the cultist some of the powers which he does claim. I suspect that this is why the Golden Dawn in its wisdom had a technique known as the 'Testing of the Spirits' which was designed to check such delusions. If the 'Adept' in question had gone on to analyse his visions as pure symbols he might have gone on to something very potent indeed, instead of trapping himself at a low level.

In looking at all these cults we might take one great exemplar of Western spirituality - the figure of Jesus - and ask ourselves: Would he teach by correspondence course? Would God reject us if we failed our monthly payments? No, if we are sincerely committed to the magical and mystical path the right people will find their ways to us in good time. While all the occult powers that cults and sensational literature promise are far less important than the question of whether the magician is, at heart, a good and kindly person.

	Inner	*Outer*
Malkuth	Magic Circles, Invocations, Creation of 'Weapons' Ritual Practices	Everyday World Home Work Employment Discrimination
Yesod	Astral Magic Evocation of Images, Far Memories, Conditioning of Consciousness	Dreams Sex Memories Self-Awareness Independence
Hod	Occult Study, Analysis, Research into Magical Techniques, Meditation	Conversation Travel Communication Reading Observing Musing
Netzach	Magical Identification, Passionate Commitment, Occult Enthusiasm Summoning of Energies	Romance High Spirits Rapture Courtship Pleasure

It will be seen, then, that there are countless levels of magical practice and training. We might draw a brief chart of these on Inner and Outer levels.

This is a very simple and off-the-cuff chart to show the different approaches to Magic in the lower Spheres, but one which is meant to imply that the outer levels are as sacred and capable of giving as much illumination as the inner. In fact one of the so-called 'Oaths' that used to be taken at a certain grade in the hierarchical structures of old systems was that we must come to view every event, action and circumstance as a direct and secret dealing between the spirit of the seeker and God. There is no reason at all why you cannot begin with this approach right away. Its value is that you can come to see your outward circumstances in a very different light than before. And if you can direct your life according to the highest qualities of the Tree, then so much the better.

Which is easier said than done, God knows.

There is no doubt that that much over-used word 'karma' plays the major part in how or when - or even where - an individual makes links with like-minded souls. A person could feel inflicted by endless runs of bad luck, difficult circumstances which are not (apparently) of his own making, and ground down by unpleasant and recurrent situations at home or work.

All that anyone can ask for in these times is justice, pure and simple. Which is why the Egyptian god Thoth, Lord of Justice, was often regarded as the most important deity, for we can bear any hardship, any loss, if we can find a reason for it, or if we can believe that we are somehow paying our debts by suffering thus; or - best of all - if we surely know that matters will be redressed in our favour before very long. If justice is being done, or will be done on our behalf, then we can endure all things.

In grave situations within your own life, then, you can call up your own Lord of Justice. Whether this is Thoth in typical Egyptian form, or an aspect of the Christ, or the Dark Goddess even, does not matter so much as that your plea is a passionate and heartfelt one. You can do this in connection with any of the foregoing rituals and techniques. The plea itself should go something like this:

> *If it is right and proper that I am being made to suffer like this, or that [N] is doing this to me, then I will try and accept it, and try to learn whatever lessons are necessary. Help me in this. But if the situation is unjust, and [N] is being completely unfair, then please redress the balance. Bring justice back into my life.*

Create your own words along these lines, in your own speech rhythms. Imagine that you are offering your problem up to the deity in question. And then sit back and wait.

The one thing you must realise is that if you are truly being made to learn some much-needed lesson in life, and if the problems *are* of your own making and no one else's, then this apparently simple magical act will bring the rest of the karmic energies through *at once*. If you were unhappy before, and cursed with seeming bad luck, then you will be staggered by what is about to come. But at least the situation will be brought to a head very fast, and you can get that karmic lesson over with more quickly than otherwise. And you *will* have a balance in your life at the end of it.

On the other hand, you may very well find that chronic problems clear up quite suddenly, that the hated [N] is given his or her comeuppance in the most appropriate way. No true magician would ever actively curse another, because he who curses always has to pay a price for such an act, one way or another. But there is no reason why we should not call down the powers of Geburah in this manner and seek that level of Justice which is everyone's right.

Chapter Ten
The Mysteries of Knowing

The early chapter on the Tree of Life briefly mentioned the sphere of Daath. We can look at this in a little more detail now because it gives us a glimpse of where humanity can go from here.

Daath means simply 'knowledge'. It is not knowledge in the intellectual, academic sense; it has nothing to do with university degrees or the ability to wrap up a simple concept in swathes of verbiage to give it a false substance. Daath is pure experience - or rather the impact that such experience has upon the psyche. When a man and a woman know each other in the old Biblical sense, then they are in touch with Daath.

Clearly Malkuth and Daath must be connected. The artist and occultist Austin Osman Spare touched on this in a crude, dark sort of way when he stated that 'Knowledge is the excrement of experience.' But then again he was a crude and dark sort of man. For polite purposes (not always the best or most effective) he might have said 'Knowledge is the residue of experience.' Or in yet other terms: Daath is the essence of Malkuth.

As the old Kabbalists were concerned to point out, Daath was not a sphere as such. 'The spheres number ten and not nine; ten and not eleven' they affirmed, because Daath was seen more as a potential, or a sense of immanence. Its traditional symbol is the Empty Room, which was the true secret of what actually lay behind the temple veil of the Holy of Holies. Daath was also the bridge across the dreaded Abyss which is so beloved of occult fiction writers.

It was the mystic and philosopher G.I. Gurdjieff who based his own spiritual system upon the notion that man has no soul, only a potential. This potential, he insisted, could be achieved only through inner work And so at one level it was the Mysteries of Daath he was touching upon.

This may become clearer when you consider the esoteric belief that Malkuth's original position upon the Tree of Life was in fact at Daath. Thus the Tree, before the Fall, would have looked like Figure 7. This points to the belief that Mankind once existed as free and blissful spirits in a perfectly harmonious universe. The disharmony was caused when these free spirits "fell into matter." Fell into Malkuth. Prior to that the lowest realms were to be found in the astral levels of Yesod, which name means Foundation, and which is seen to be exactly that upon what might be called the Perfected Tree.

Daath can therefore be regarded as 'Inner Earth.' All of those spiritual systems which posit the living consciousness of the land and embrace the notion that we can be united with the land in a magically symbiotic relationship are linked with the Daath revelation.

We experience, and thus we *know*.

Link with the consciousness of the Earth beneath, and we can *know* things that will help us touch the stars.

In this respect the magic of Daath is linked with the images of caves (or sometimes tunnels) within sacred mountains. In the latter case we find outstanding lumps of the densest matter which humans look to for heavenly salvation. Such mountains are found in every country, among every race. In almost all cases local myth also links them with mystic caves buried deep within. These caves are held to contain hero figures, or treasures of a magical, talismanic nature. Entering such caves invariably transforms those who find their way in.

Of course this is a clear echo of the Kabbalistic symbol of the Empty Room which yet conceals the greatest of secrets. And modern life being what it is, occult literature of a certain kind abounds with tales of mysterious caves in mystic mountains which contain artifacts of stellar origin - advanced technologies

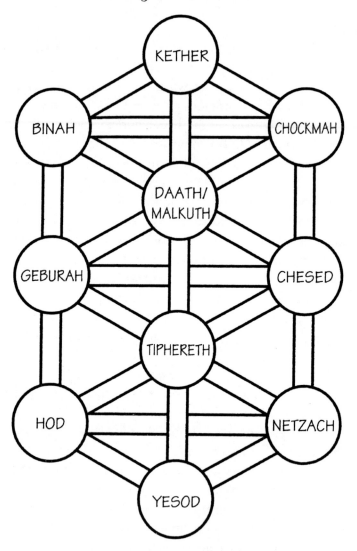

Figure 6 The Perfected Tree

from the most distant past. Writers such as Bulwer-Lytton, George Hunt Williamson, Erich von Daniken and Lobsang Rampa (to name just a few) have all touched upon this theme in different ways, although in truth we should not take any of them too seriously.

In this respect there is a hill near me which is said to be the home of Puck, the King of the Fairies. It was linked with the Knights Templar in medieval times. It is said to be hollow and contain the golden figure of a sacred ram. All of these things and more were said before the Space Age began. Now it is seen as the focus of massive UFO activity and is believed by some to contain a homing beacon for these craft, which some observers insist come from *within* the hill.

All of the latter are myths for our time, as C.G. Jung observed. In previous centuries men and women were 'carried off' by fairies or demons. Now they are abducted by extra-terrestrials. All part of the Mysteries of Daath if we but knew it.

Long before the present penchant for alien abductions (and let it be said now that hypnotic regressions 'proving' the latter are probably the most inaccurate, deceptive, and largely useless techniques in the spiritual repertoire) long before these became popular, magicians were making active use of the 'Cave in the Mountain' imagery. My book *Dancers to the Gods* contains the diaries of Charles Seymour from the late 1930s, in which this genuine Adept describes his contact with the inner-plane entity known as Cheiron, an otherworld being who helped him write *The Old Religion*. As an essay on self-initiation into the Pagan mysteries of what was termed the 'Green Ray', this has yet to be surpassed According to Seymour this entity Cheiron had (and has) an evolutionary interest in humanity, and was linked - obviously - with the star-system of Alpha Centauri. Obviously because Cheiron was, in mythological terms, the leader of all the centaurs according to Greek tales. The information and energies that Seymour channeled from Cheiron was of a very high order indeed, but, more important for our present purposes, contains all the themes of Man and Nature linking with the stars by means of an empty space within a holy mountain.

When Seymour visualised that cave within his imagination, and in a very real sense entered therein to meet Cheiron, he *knew* that this was a genuine experience in another dimension. But the important thing is that none of us needs to accept this on trust. We must find our *own* knowing, our own gnosis. We must experience the world of matter in our own way, as already stated, and draw energies into that Empty Room or Mystic Cave which lies within our own psyches.

We can make a beginning by using any of the ritual or imaginative techniques already described to prepare clear conditions for a Working. If you already know of a sacred mountain, or site of any kind which appeals to you (and don't worry about anyone else) then either go there - literally - or build it up in your imagination as intensely as possible. If you are actually there then make simple acknowledgments to the resident spirits, and then to the Elements, before visualising a cave buried deep within the earth. Visualise yourself stepping out of your body and making your way through the ground toward it. If you are unable to be there in the flesh then visualise a narrow road leading to the place in question, rising gradually to a mid-point on the mountain slopes. Visualise a narrow fissure where your rocky path ends. Step through this and on and down a long, subterranean passageway which gleams with its own light. Try to sense the massive weight of the rock and minerals around you, increasing as you descend. At the end of the passage see a heavy and impossibly ancient door, bearing the symbol of the equi-armed circle-cross which is the oldest (and safest) of all images, and notice the brilliant shafts of light which spear out from the gaps between the door and its frame. Pause, take a breath, and open that door...

This and many variations of the same has become almost a standard technique for making a direct link with what some might call Guides, others Guardians, and others still 'inner contacts.' It is impossible to say what you will see. It may be no more than a radiance with a very strong sense of presence behind it, which may or may not make its identity clear with further contacts. It may be something visually startling, such as a clear and very real image of whatever entity looks after the seeker's best interests. Or else nothing very much may *seem* to happen at all. But even in the latter case as a new magician you are still expanding your consciousness and experience by your very effort, and this will come to have effects that will only gradually become apparent. The Empty Room within the psyche will start to sparkle. Gnosis will begin.

The foregoing technique can be bolstered if the magician can procure or bring back an actual piece of rock from the sacred place in question. After that, no matter where he might be in geographical terms, he can always put himself in touch with his power-source - quite literally - holding the stone while working at the purely visual techniques described.

Failing that, crystal is a wondrous aid. The magician can mentally project the image of the sacred mountain into the crystal and carry on the Working as given. Failing *that*, you can use a smoke-blackened mirror, or a bowl of dark liquid, or any of the traditional scrying aids to effect entry into this Cave.

It is while you do Work of this nature that you sometimes touch upon the highest aspects of talismanic magic, although these can often distract you from the true nature of Daath. and cause the Empty Room to become very cluttered indeed. It is the knowledge that matter is, or can be, imbued with spiritual energy. That lumps of crystal, for example, can help to transform us from within. In another area the practice of alchemy sought to transmute base matter into gold and bring the alchemist to immortality along the way. And although modern scientific knowledge discourages most people from practicing this art today, there is no reason why they could not, for example, create a system based upon home wine-making! The stages of fermentation can be made to parallel the traditional alchemical stages exactly; the act of gathering the raw material from a particular holy site at a particular time can be made into a Wiccan-type act in its own right. And at the end of it the alchemist *will* actually have something which can (legally) alter consciousness for sacerdotal purposes. When I did it myself using dandelions from the foot of Glastonbury Tor, my purpose was not to achieve the Philosopher's Stone, so much as to become Philosopher Stoned, in the most genteel of senses. In truth the wine I made was dreadful but the experience of making it was something else.

The Mysteries of Daath are perhaps more closely entwined with the concept of Time than those of any other sphere. As Henri Bergson wrote 'Time is the ratio of the resistance of Matter to Spirit.' When the two are united we become outside of Time. In an area of consciousness where Time does not exist. A space between the worlds which parallels the cave within the Mountain.

There is one level in which we can regard this space as the gap between what we are, and what we *know* we should be. It is the gap between what our mortal warps and quirks compel us to persist in being, and that which our inner spark is quite certain we could be. Most of us spend a lifetime trying to cross that gap, or in despair because we do not know how, or else are afraid to try. All of this, on a purely psychological level, is but a lower analogue of that dreaded Abyss in which the evil and the nightmares of the entire universe can be found, and which Daath is said to straddle.

So at the simplest level the Mysteries of Daath teach us how to cross the gap between where we are, spiritually, and where we will to be, by the act of knowing ourselves. By holding firm to whatever self-gnosis we achieve, we can pluck up the courage to traverse our own nightmares. We can get closer to the Source.

This gap, this Abyss, also has another function which Austin Spare hinted at in the earlier mentioned quote, and which William G. Gray states quite explicitly in his *Ladder of Lights*, in which he shows the Abyss to find its physical parallel in humans within the eliminative system. That is, there is a psycho-spiritual function within us which is quite able to break down bad memories and personal trauma in such a way as they can be, in effect, excreted from our system. Used accordingly, such waste matter will find its own place, ultimately providing a fertilizer that can benefit everyone. Modern psychology, unable or unwilling to accept the necessity or possibility of such a function, is all too often guilty of reaching into shit, and trying to reconstitute it.

This may sound grim, or disturbing, but the process of knowing yourself must necessarily take in some truly abysmal revelations. In the old tradition this gap/crack/abyss - call it what you will - could be traversed by walking over a Bridge of Swords, the latter themselves being known as the Swords of Truth. In brief, truth hurts. Self-truth most of all. We can get all cut up. And if we are not mercilessly honest with ourselves, if we are not fearless and extremely well balanced, then we can fall in and spend the rest of our life wallowing.

No, it really isn't easy. Which is why we need some help from those entities on the other side who have our evolutionary interests at heart.

Chapter 11
Egyptian Magic

hen we begin to put all these themes and techniques together for the first time, and perhaps try to take steps away from the Judaeo-Christian emphasis of the traditional Kabbalah, it is often easier to start off using the Egyptian system. Not that the techniques themselves bear any resemblance to that which would have been practised during the Pyramid Age, for example, but because the energies involved present themselves via imagery which has become almost universalised over the millennia. Besides which the Egyptian deities had such specific forms that they are actually quite easy to visualise. In contrast, the spirit of Baldur, for example, may have vast appeal for the intending practitioner of the Norse tradition, but his actual appearance is a matter for individual whim. For the novice, attempts to assume such a god-form often result in a kind of fuzziness and uncertainty which can detract from the rest of the exercise. But with Egyptian Magic, as it has been developed over the past century at least, the lines and colours and postures of the deities can be seen in countless sources, with only minor variations.

The Ka Posture

You can begin with the *ka* posture. It involves no more than standing with feet together and arms raised as in Figure 8. Now done in such a spiritless fashion the *ka* posture is an empty little exercise. But you can fill it with great energy with surprising ease.

By simple and subtle alterations of the hands (i.e. by making them clenched or open, facing upward or forward,

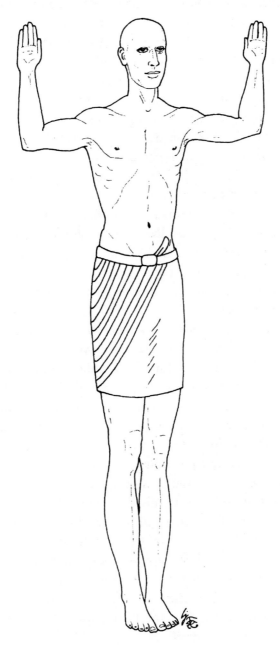

Figure 7 The K a Posture (Illustrated by Billie John)

straight or tilted), you can make the ka posture express rage or victory, supplication or surrender. Sportsmen constantly and unconsciously express the *ka* posture when they have won their event, and are in the throes of exultation. With only the simplest changes the same gesture is used by soldiers surrendering. Someone who has had great and unexpected luck will often glance upward and fling his arms likewise in a *ka* posture of thanks to the deity responsible.

Try a variety of such postures, varying the angle and inclination of the arms and the body, adopting the appropriate mannerisms for each emotion. But at the same time try to feel the emotion concerned: triumph or delight, pleading, yearning, or perhaps even divine submission to a greater Will than yours. Great actors and magicians do this sort of thing all the time, for the two crafts are closely linked.

After a while, you can learn to synchronise this with a breathing exercise.

Adopt as elegant a stance as you can, one hand resting lightly on top of the other at the level of your groin. At first do no more than stand there for a little while breathing regularly and deeply (though not unnaturally so). Then take a slow and deeper breath and bring your hands up to the level of your solar plexus, at the same time visualising a column of pure brilliance being brought up from the base of your spine. Breathe out, but keep your hands and the column of light in the same place. Then breathe in again and bring your hands and the light up to the level of your throat this time, your thumbs linked as though forming the symbol of a bird in shadow-play. And finally at the third breath raise your hands into the *ka* posture itself while seeing the light carry on into your head and indeed spinning out from the crown during your exhalation.

Sometimes the light takes on a real inner intensity during the exhalation rather than the inhalation. Try it and decide what feels right for yourself.

The fountaining light can be seen to spray out into the shape of the auric egg as described in the Exercise of the Middle Pillar in an earlier chapter. And at this point similar work can be done in terms of colour visualisation and energy projection.

Once a degree of mastery has been achieved with this, we can also build into it exercises relating to the endocrine system. As detailed in *The Inner Guide to Egypt*, written by myself and B. Walker-John, the Ancient Egyptians truly believed that their country was an earthly mirror for the heavens above, and that Man was an expression of them both. That is to say certain Mystery Centres of Ancient Egypt could be seen as earthly analogues of certain stellar energies; while at the same time these earthly and stellar centres found direct equivalents within the endocrine glands of similar function.

Thus starting at the bottom, the testes or ovaries would equate with the energies of Thebes; the pancreas would relate to the Mysteries of Abydos; the adrenal glands linked with Hermopolis; the thymus with Memphis; the thyroid and parathyroid with Heliopolis; the pineal with Khebit; and lastly the pituitary with Alexandria.

The actual Egyptian names of these places can then be turned into 'Words of Power' which are no less effective than the Hebrew god-names used in traditional Kabbalistic exercises.

(For the sake of the present exercise, and for reasons that we cannot detail here, the pituitary and pineal can be energised at the same time as the thyroid.)

Centre	Egyptian Name
Thebes	Uas (*Wass or Wast*)
Abydos	Abtu
Hermopolis	Khemnu
Memphis	Men-nefer
Heliopolis	Aunu

Visualise these centres on your body as jewels which glow accordingly when the rising light touches them. Synchronise your breathing as you see fit. You need not worry about exact pronunciations of each word, or exact patterns of inhalation. Just work at it, and find what works best for you.

Astral Masks

Again, in time, a new phase can be introduced in this exercise of the *ka* posture, and one which involves the donning of astral masks as a preliminary to assuming the full god-form.

What you must do first is find any book which may contain details of the Egyptian gods and goddesses. Read as much as possible about their functions. Horus, for example, can be seen in simple terms as the young warrior god, champion of light, destroyer of darkness. Assuming the appropriate *ka* posture for these qualities, then visualise also the Horus hawk head upon yourself. Not just as a convenient addition to your own cranium, but an actual transformation of yourself. Do this while intoning the name Heru (the true version of Horus) in whatever manner is most resonant.

Men or women can do this exercise, although the latter may prefer the vulture-goddess of Mut, or the lion-goddess Sekhmet, who had great powers of healing as well as a willingness to tear apart anyone who might harm her children.

The same work can be done with Anubis, the jackal-god known as the Opener of the Way whose metabolism is able to derive spiritual energies from what others might see as dead meat; in other words, bright wisdom from the most dismal experience.

Osiris, the fertility god, is invariably human in form but he wears the splendid headpiece, the atef.-crown, which proclaims him as Lord of the Underworld and also a Horned God. His true name is Asar.

All of the strange animal or bird heads, all of the headpieces, such as the vulture wings or crescent moon, all of these provide sharp and easily visualised symbols that we can build into our self-imagery as we use the *ka* posture.

Figure 8. The Ka statue of King Auibre' Hor of the 13th Dynasty from his tomb at Dahsur (Illustrated by Billie Walker John).

Isis   Horus

Ptah   Sekhmet

Ra   Thoth

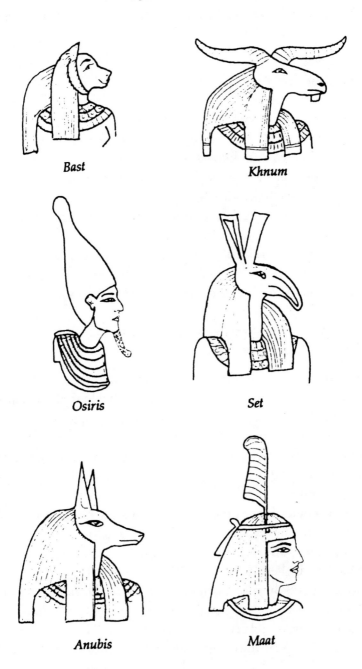

Bast

Khnum

Osiris

Set

Anubis

Maat

We can also begin to ask ourselves the same series of questions that we described earlier:

Have you ever felt young and vigorous and a champion of truth and fair play? Then you can link with Horus.
Have you ever held down a good job and built up a home? Then you can know Isis- whose true name is Aset.
Have you ever made anything grow? (No need to be too literal here.) Then you can know Osiris.
Have you ever kept yourself to yourself and revelled in secrets? You can make links with Nephthys.
Have you ever experienced death and gained insights from it? You can make contact with Sokaris.
Have you ever gained personal power from confronting the dark aspects of your psyche? Then you can know Anubis.
Have you ever tried bringing order into a chaotic situation? Then you can link with Maat.
Have you ever enjoyed knowledge for the sake of knowledge? Then you can know Thoth.

And on and on and on, throughout the massed pantheons of a lost realm which still exists within us. A vital part of the magic is actually learning how to ask ourselves these questions.

If we wish to tie all of this in with the aforementioned imagery of the Kabbalah itself, perhaps by associating the Egyptian deities with the Spheres, then there is infinite scope for the individual.

One could, for example, decide to work with the Sphere of the Moon, known in the Kabbalah as Yesod, but which would in the Egyptian scheme fit in quite nicely with Thebes, and the Moon-gods there, as well as with the ovaries, the Mysteries of Women, and the months of the year. Using the Tarot card The Moon as a gateway you could visualise yourself going between the two towers and across the brow of the hill into the Temple of Mut, the great vulture goddess whose name is actually a root for 'mother,' and whose temple was once fronted by a sacred

lake shaped like the embryo in the womb. No need to give
here one of those path-workings which are so often merely an
excuse for the writer to indulge in purple prose. If Mut wants
you, if she has any resonance at all within your psyche, she will
be more than happy to help you create a very real path of your
own toward her.

The main thing to bear in mind, always, is that it is just as
unwise to mix magical systems as it is to mix drinks. If you
decide to fashion something along Egyptian lines, it should
not involve archangels from the particular Sphere concerned,
or use Hebrew 'Names of Power.'

The framework of the Tree of Life is in itself neutral (as is
the Tarot to a large extent), but if you want to build it up with
Egyptian imagery or whatever, then when you begin to work
through it you must learn to switch off from the traditional
version before switching onto whatever frequencies you have
now decided to use. Which is why, although the Egyptian
'centres' in the *ka* posture have direct parallels with the Hebrew
Sephirah, we do not use the god-names of the latter to energise
the former. In fact, if the original Egyptian names had not
been known then it would have been better for you to make
up nonsense sonics of your own. Just as ridiculous nicknames
between lovers can take on real meaning and influence between
the people concerned, so can fanciful sounds be used for the
highest magical purposes.

Chapter 12
Past Lives Revisited

One of the things which invariably happens when a person begins and sustains magical work, is that circumstances arise, dreams or visions develop, which seem to indicate the certainty of a past life. Of course, one of the immediate criticisms provoked by all those antagonistic to the whole magical process is that such experiences are no more than compensatory boosts to the ego. Without having the slightest experience of such things themselves, or of any intimacy with genuine practitioners of the art, they invariably invoke names like Cleopatra or Napoleon to poke fun and give themselves an air of detached wisdom.

While there certainly are inadequate individuals who do seek to gain substance by claiming to have been someone exalted from history, these same individuals could never undergo real magical training. They would make these claims however their lives progressed. In practice, however, none of the genuine Adepts of my acquaintance have ever shown any great interest in who they may have been in earlier epochs. They were (and are) too busy getting on with their Work in this life to be hooked on past lives. Only Christine Hartley, whose far memories are adequately recorded in my *Dancers to the Gods,* gave a reasonably exalted identity as Merit-aten, a princess from Ancient Egypt. But it was a matter of supreme indifference to her whether anyone else believed her, and her everyday life was extraordinary enough as it was, without taking into account her magic. And as she herself said, princesses in Ancient Egypt were a dime a dozen. It was no great deal.

Even so, the topic of reincarnation is by no means as simple as the standard philosophy would seem to suggest. There is no doubt that 'far memories' gained from hypnotic regression are always immensely detailed, and emotionally convincing, but tests have shown again and again how inaccurate those details really are. That is not to say that *all* hypnotic regressions are no more than visionary deceptions, but they are best admired as demonstrations of the mind's wonderful ability to create cohesive epics that are essentially fictional in nature. This does not mean that we cannot get wisdom and delight from such things. But no one should never never *never* accept that a thing has been 'proved' because it was demonstrated by the process of hypnotic regression.

Quite often, also, a person can tune in to past events in the most unexpected circumstances. Such events can replay themselves before his inner vision with immense lucidity. This is the idea that certain places can retain their own memories, stored away within the stones like on a videotape, and spontaneously replaying themselves to the astonished inner gaze of particular souls. The latter may experience these so intensely that the assumption is made of having gone through these events in a past life. It may well be so, but there is also the possibility to consider that he was acting as no more than a receiving apparatus.

Yet another possibility which can affect the whole experience of 'far memory' is the fact that when a magician makes contact with an inner-plane entity of historical fact, images and experiences of the entity will often filter through into the magician's consciousness. Often, he can be tempted to think he was that entity in question. It is a natural temptation. Everyone succumbs to it for a little while in the early phases of magical work.

All of which can go toward explaining why the gods are supposed to destroy whoever becomes guilty of hubris, or overwhelming pride. It is never because the gods feel challenged, and thus determined to humble the wretch concerned. It is because hubris stops the magician from becoming a clear and effective channel for their energies. The magician can no longer do the Work as it should be done. So the gods withdraw and leave him to deal with their echoes and shells only; and soon the man destroys himself.

When the magician first plugs into what might be termed a 'Magical Current' - which, like Time, is experienced but almost impossible to define - external events occur which seem to be clear examples of some cosmic power sending signs to confirm the veracity of the contact. These events often take the form of reincarnation sagas involving groups of people.

For example, in the early 70s I began work on an as yet unpublished novel based around the isle of Lindisfarne in the 7th century. Lindisfarne is an island only a mile off the northeast coast of England, reachable twice a day by road when the tide recedes, and regarded by many as one of the major power-centres of Britain. Historically it ranks alongside Iona as one of the last bastions of Celtic Christianity, was the source of the dazzling and illuminated Lindisfarne Gospels, and was seen to keep the light of Civilization flickering at a time when it was going out all over Europe. No sooner had I started writing than people began to appear in the most unlikely and unexpected ways, all of whom had Lindisfarne fascinations for the same period. The name itself would crop up in every conceivable source: in newspapers, magazines, on television documentaries, or on the radio via the songs of the once famous folk-rock group of that name. Always appearing at apparently crucial or significant moments, though often in the most insignificant ways, and always with a staggering frequency of occurrence.

On and on this went, a saga involving incredible levels of coincidence, drawing in many people who became as surprised as myself, the events and their omens circling around my own life constantly, but never quite linking up in any solid mandala of revelation.

My conclusion at that time was that I had once been a monk on Lindisfarne and that the rest of the events could be explained by the concept of group reincarnation. Really it was a delicious time. For a number of years I lived with the notion that once, in the Dark Ages, I had been a monk on a tiny island amid the grey sea with seals and gulls for company.

However, I eventually had to admit the historical details which presented themselves in a variety of ways were wrong. Sure, they possessed enough half-truth and quasi-possibility to lead me down many false paths, but at the end of the day there was no avoiding the fact that they were wrong. End of story.

As far as I can explain it now (and explanations are not always wise or necessary) the act of brooding upon Lindisfarne acted like the touch upon the keyboard of some cosmic computer. The computer itself, which exists in all dimensions, did no more than display before me all the references it had on that topic, doing so in a multitude of experiential ways even though the references (like identical names in a telephone directory) did not necessarily bear any relationship to each other.

Not so much egg on the face as ego on the face, but every magician goes through this sort of thing. It is enthralling while it lasts. The only danger lies in getting hooked on the twists and turns of the apparent saga, rather than concentrating on the energy behind it.

Yet over and above all of these 'explanations' for what seems to be reincarnation, many people still do have experiences in which they know to their bones that they have lived before in a particular place at a particular time. This knowledge can be so intense, so impossible to articulate, that the person concerned has no compulsion to tell anyone else, no burning desire to seek documentary proof. Knowing with all your heart can be enough.

Personally I believe that while reincarnation of the classical kind does occur, it is by no means universal. We are not all guaranteed a return. I believe that it does happen in the case

Figure 11. *Kha'n-uas*. *(Illustrations by Billie Walker John).*

of sudden or violent death. Or else when the magician or mystic concerned is so closely attuned in his own lifetime to his own Higher Self.

As I have written elsewhere, quoting the words of Charles Seymour, a personality incarnates but never reincarnates. It is the Higher Self which does so, sending little bits of itself into incarnation each time in order to gain experience. Thus a particular Higher Self (regard it as a group mind/soul, or superconscious corporate entity) can have numerous souls in incarnation at any one time - even extending *through* time. It is perhaps not so much that we have previous lives, as *other* lives. Like the beads on a necklace, all connected by the same thread. Glimpses we may have of what seem to be previous lives can often be other aspects of our own Higher Self as they exist in a different time. Parts of ourselves, in fact. We are one another, all over again.

To this extent I believe that a part of myself once existed (or exists) in the 19th Dynasty of Ancient Egypt as a junior scribe. Also that this link helped Billie John and I to bring through that relatively complete and 'new' magical system described in our *Inner Guide to Egypt*. All of which was under the aegis of the entity shown in Figure 11.

But if all this could somehow be disproved tomorrow it would cause me no devastation at all. Life is too short for that.

Techniques for Recall

The best book ever written on past life recall is by Christine Hartley's pupil, Judy Hall, whose *Deja Who?* takes in all the of possibilities, and shows how we can make them work for us, even if the memories or visions are not necessarily historically sound. All of this said and done, it is human nature to try and stimulate what may or may not be genuine far memories of a genuine past life. Christine Hartley reached a stage toward the end of her life where she simply created a blank screen before her mind's eye and asked her inner contacts to show her what she wanted or needed to know.

The trick behind this at one level is to act like we do when we play games with very young children, watching them while pretending not to. It helps to concentrate on the breath as it goes in and out of our nostrils, visualising it as pure light, while at the same time keeping the inner gaze lightly upon the blank screen. Pictures arise with surprising ease but these are quickly broken if the startled viewer turns his full consciousness onto them. Again, they are not necessarily from past lives. They may not be more than the astral equivalent of junk mail. This is why a preliminary invocation to whatever entity the magician thinks appropriate should be used.

Many of the visualisation techniques are akin to path-workings. You can add a simple piece of tactile back-up here by making your own Mobius Strip. This is made by taking a narrow length of paper and bringing the two ends together to form a loop. Just before you do so, however, give one of the ends a half twist and then join them up. If you study this loop you will find that it actually has become a figure with one side. Inside and outside has ceased to exist. A continuous pencil line can be drawn around it without having to take the point off the paper. The visualisation techniques can be run through while the magician sits quietly running this through his fingers like a trans-dimensional rosary.

The fingers will be reminding the subconscious that ultimately there is no outer and no inner, no past and no future, and that they are all one. The imaginative faculty, meanwhile, can be working through whatever sequence of visualisations have been chosen, although at a certain point you should keep the fingers still upon the loop-over point and just hold the Mobius Strip.

The visualisation itself could go something like this...

Picture yourself standing outside your body looking at yourself as you sit or lie in a relaxed, secure manner. Then imagine yourself shrinking into a tiny pinpoint of light, shrinking into your essence. As Aleister Crowley once said, 'Every Man and Woman is a Star,' and you might think of your essence as being like this, with your body vast before you.

Close up on your own face. See it filling your whole vision, the pores like craters. See the *ajna chakra* (the third eye) like a whirling, multi-coloured vortex. Feel the auric currents around your body rising and falling like the sea as you breathe in and out. Then, with an act of will, move into the ajna's vortex, spinning around and down, into your own forehead and the velvet night of the brain cavity.

We all know what the brain actually looks like. Look up an illustration after reading this and fix upon the main parts. Picture it like an asteroid in the depths of interstellar space. A lump of living rock lined and fissured. Circle it. Be aware of the two halves. Look at the cerebrum and cerebellum. It is in the latter, tucked away on the underside, that our minute and concentrated spark of consciousness must go. Float to the front of the cerebellum and see the great mass of the rest of the brain above. See one of the lines between the convolutions open out into a crack, and then a clear opening. Head into it, toward the heart of the cerebellum itself, twisting and turning through what seems like a maze. Here, in the middle of the most ancient part of the brain, find yourself in a crystalline cave, the walls of which you just know can reflect images from your own ancestral memories at least, and perhaps beyond these to something else again.

Ask whatever higher power you cleave to for permission to see what needs to be seen. And then wait...

Whatever happens, whatever you experience, as always return by the same route and then write down whatever you remember, no matter how trivial this may seem.

Such techniques as the latter are more effective when done with the help of someone, preferably of the opposite sex, holding hands and having one partner narrating the journey

and the other experiencing it. In reality not everyone is able
to find such a willing partner, and their spouses, no matter
how loving and supportive they might be in other areas, are
not necessarily in sympathy with this aspect of their partners'
natures. Yet there is a simple and undemanding party trick by
which anyone can demonstrate to themselves, and others, the
ease with which visions can be made to arise. Once done, the
intending magician can then approach his or her own path-
workings with a new sense of confidence.

At any small, congenial gathering, where there are no
major distractions, you can offer to demonstrate a five minute
psychoanalysis to any willing volunteer. This can be done
at a dinner table or sprawled around the living room - the
more casual the circumstance the better. Insist upon the light-
hearted nature of the experiment. Do not try to drag in occult
overtones. Tell the rest of the party that they can participate
also as long as they keep quiet, and wait until afterward to share
their own experiences. Tell the volunteer that he need simply
sit back and listen while you present to him the outline of an
imaginary journey, marked by various stages, all of which can
yield to psychological interpretations which you will describe
later.

1. Tell the volunteer to imagine that he is in a wood. Ask
him what sort of wood it is (i.e. dark and menacing, light
and cheery, deciduous or evergreen, etc.). Ask him what
season it is. What he can see as he looks around. Then
ask him how he feels about being there in the wood. Is
he happy? Intimidated? Anxious?
(What invariably happens is that the imagery builds up
with such strength that you will not need to 'lead' the
person at all, just ask him questions so that you can get
a good idea of what he is seeing.)
2. Tell him that there is a path stretching before him.
Again, get him to describe the path.
3. As he now walks along this path tell him that he finds

a key lying on the ground before him. Get him to pick this up and describe it, as before.

4. Further along he finds a cup. Question as before.

5. Further still he comes to a clearing in the middle of which is a massive and extremely menacing bear. Tell him that he has to get to the other side somehow. Get him to describe how he will do this, in any way that he wants.

6. He then comes to a body of water. Question as before. Ask him how he plans to get across it.

7. On the other side is a wall which he soon comes to. It stretches from one side of the world to the other, as far as the eye can see. Propped against it is a ladder. Get the volunteer to climb the ladder and describe what he sees on the other side.

End of party game.

Now insist at this point that the interpretations which you will give are for fun only (and they are), and most certainly not to be taken seriously.

Thus the wood will represent how the volunteer views his life at the moment - cheery or scary, dark or delightful, wintry or in full summer. The path through it a symbol of how he sees his own progress, whether this is via muddy twists and turns, getting nowhere, or on a broad dry path. The key is a symbol of the ego - small or massive, bright or dull. The cup, a symbol of the emotional state. How a person deals with the bear in the clearing is a symbol of how he tends to confront problems - head on, or sneaking around the side. The body of water is a symbol of the sex drive. The wall on the other side is a symbol of death, and of what a person might expect to see on the other side.

It cannot be emphasised too strongly here that this is a light-hearted game, no more, best done among friends after a few glasses of wine. When the Welsh poet David Annwn did this to me many years ago (and this is always a one-off) my key was a massive device, bigger than a bazooka, which I could scarcely lift; my cup was a filthy cracked affair, disgusting inside; I hid from the bear and skirted around it; my body of water was a massive, seething lake, boiling with ichthyosaurii and other primitive creatures, which I crossed on the smallest of boats while giving Tarzan calls; but beyond the wall I saw ... marvellous things.

It is a laugh, no more (and what is wrong with that?); but after you've played this game a few times you can get a real sense of the possibilities behind true magical path-workings, such as you might find in *The Shining Paths** by Dolores Ashcroft-Nowicki, which is effectively an experiential exploration of the Tree of Life using its deepest symbolism. You can then go on with some confidence to fashion something for yourself that may or may not involve others. As will happen with such magic, the effectiveness of this party game develops as you think of the best ways to put it across to each person. No good reading from a script. No good being ponderous or pompous. Do it with friends, for the friendliest of purposes, and work your magic likewise.

The true disciplines of magic are never easy, as I've said time and time again, but there is no reason why we should not have a little fun along the way. And if you can't occasionally learn to poke fun at yourself, then don't even bother making the journey inward.

*Published by Thoth Publications

Chapter 13
Conclusion

By now you will have within your grasp the essential techniques which form the backbone of the Western Magical Tradition as it has existed for most of this century and a little before. You can banish unpleasant atmospheres, purify places of working, build patterns in your aura and create gates into other dimensions. Your task now is to use these techniques and improve upon them, thus making sure that this same Tradition in a century's time has gone on at least a few steps. Never get bogged down by dogma, or timidity; set no limits on your imagination. Work your magic with all the passion, elegance, and basic human decency that you can command.

Appendix

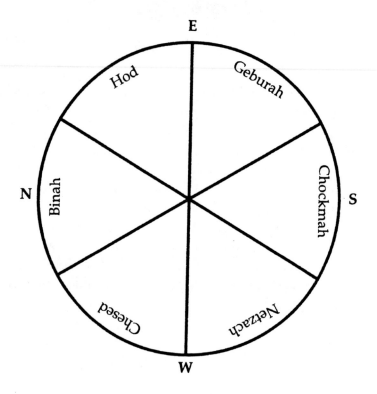

Figure 12

This is just one interpretation of the Tree as arranged on the circle-cross. The Spheres of the Middle Pillar are held to form a central axis with Tiphereth at the centre and, if we imagine that we are looking down upon a spherical shape, Kether at the top pole with Yesod at the bottom. Malkuth is the whole thing in itself.

There are other variations of course, but this is one of the least inelegant. One of the variations would hold to the above pattern but add Malkuth with Binah; Kether with Hod and Geburah; Tiphereth in the south with Chockmah; and Yesod to the west. Choose for yourself.

Traditional Correspondences

Kether

Mundane Chakra	-------
Archangel	Metatron
God-Name	Eheieh
Magical Image	The face of a bearded patriarch shown in profile
Colour	Brilliance
Symbols	The point within a circle, the node of the cosmic lemniscates, the crown

Chockmah

Mundane Chakra	The zodiac
Archangel	Ratziel
God-Name	Jehovah, Yahweh, Yod He Vau Heh
Magical Image	A bearded male figure, full face
Colour	Iridescent grey, flecked with light
Symbols	The straight line, the phallus, the rod

Binah

Mundane Chakra	Saturn
Archangel	Tzaphkiel
God-Name	Jehovah Elohim
Magical Image	A mature woman
Colour	Black, dark hues
Symbols	The cup, the lamp

Chesed

Mundane Chakra	Jupiter
Archangel	Tsadkiel
God-Name	El
Magical Image	A benevolent king enthroned
Colour	Blue
Symbol	The square, the cornucopia, laughter

Geburah

Mundane Chakra	Mars
Archangel	Khamael
God-Name	Elohim Gibor
Magical Image	A stern king in his chariot
Colour	Red
Symbols	The scourge, the sword, the pentagon

Tiphereth

Mundane Chakra	The Sun
Archangel	Michael
God-Name	Jehovah Aloah va Daas
Magical Image	A child, a priest-king, a sacrificed god
Colour	Salmon-pink gold flecked
Symbols	The hexagram, the rose

Netzach

Mundane Chakra	Venus
Archangel	Auriel

God-Name	JHVH Tzawem
Magical Image	A beautiful, naked female
Colour	Emerald
Symbols	The girdle. the seven-pointed star

Hod

Mundane Chakra	Mercury
Archangel	Raphael
God-Name	Elohim Tzavoos
Magical Image	A hermaphrodite
Colour	Orange-yellow
Symbols	The caduceus, the serpent

Yesod

Mundane Chakra	The Moon
Archangel	Gabriel
God-Name	Shaddaiel Chaiim
Magical Image	A powerful, naked man
Colour	Violet-blue
Symbols	The cup, the mirror

Malkuth

Mundane Chakra	Earth
Archangel	Sandalphon
Cod-Name	Adonai ha Aretz
Magical Image	A crowned queen (Nature)
Colour	Citrine, olive, russet. black
Symbols	Sandals, the altar

Useful Books

Books often seem to have their own innate power to make themselves appear when we need them. They come looking for us, even if we are completely unaware of them. Nowadays you have the marvellous internet search engines to help you go much further than we ever could. Even so, here are a few suggestions for worthwhile further reading.

The Mystical Qabalah by Dion Fortune is still the best book ever written on that subject. 'Dion Fortune' was the pen name of a woman who died in 1946, and whose importance as a writer, magician, and visionary is only now being recognised. Her two novels *The Sea Priestess* and *Moon Magic* are without compare, and teach more about real magic than most technical books can ever hope to achieve. Among many other books she also wrote that curious and often intensely beautiful book *Psychic Self-Defence*, which is more a magical autobiography than anything else, and which gives numerous practical methods of proven effectiveness.

Those people who would like to go further into the QBL itself should read W.G. Gray's *Ladder of Lights*, which looks at the Tree from a completely different angle, and which is appropriately subtitled *Kabbalah Renovata*. David Godwin's excellent *Cabalistic Encyclopaedia* provides a dictionary of Kabbalism as understood and interpreted by the various Hermetic societies of the West.

Israel Regardie's *Foundations of Practical Magic* contains his long essay 'The Art of True Healing' which gave the first exposition of the Middle Pillar Exercise. *The Magician -His Training* and Work by W.E. Butler has an atmosphere all its own.

In the realms of ritual magic pure and simple, there is the immensely practical *Temple Magic* by W.G. Gray again, and the *Ritual Magic Workbook* by Dolores Ashcroft-Nowicki.

These are suggestions only. In truth, the books you will most need are probably already making their cunning ways toward you, if they haven't already done so.

Other titles from Thoth Publications

AN INTRODUCTION TO RITUAL MAGIC
By Dion Fortune & Gareth Knight

At the time this was something of a unique event in esoteric publishing - a new book by the legendary Dion Fortune. Especially with its teachings on the theory and practice of ritual or ceremonial magic, by one who, like the heroine of two of her other novels, was undoubtedly "a mistress of that art".

In this work Dion Fortune deals in successive chapters with Types of Mind Working; Mind Training; The Use of Ritual; Psychic Perception; Ritual Initiation; The Reality of the Subtle Planes; Focusing the Magic Mirror; Channelling the Forces; The Form of the Ceremony; and The Purpose of Magic - with appendices on Talisman Magic and Astral Forms.

Each chapter is supplemented and expanded by a companion chapter on the same subject by Gareth Knight. In Dion Fortune's day the conventions of occult secrecy prevented her from being too explicit on the practical details of magic, except in works of fiction. These veils of secrecy having now been drawn back, Gareth Knight has taken the opportunity to fill in much practical information that Dion Fortune might well have included had she been writing today.

In short, in this unique collaboration of two magical practitioners and teachers, we are presented with a valuable and up-to-date text on the practice of ritual or ceremonial magic "as it is". That is to say, as a practical, spiritual, and psychic discipline, far removed from the lurid superstition and speculation that are the hall mark of its treatment in sensational journalism and channels of popular entertainment.

ISBN 1-870450 31 0 Deluxe Hardback Limited edition
ISBN 1-870450 26 4 Soft cover edition

DION FORTUNE AND THE INNER LIGHT

By Gareth Knight

At last – a comprehensive biography of Dion Fortune based upon the archives of the Society of the Inner Light. As a result much comes to light that has never before been revealed. This includes:

Her early experiments in trance mediumship with her Golden Dawn teacher Maiya Curtis-Webb and in Glastonbury with Frederick Bligh Bond, famous for his psychic investigations of Glastonbury Abbey.

The circumstances of her first contact with the Masters and reception of "The Cosmic Doctrine" The ambitious plans of the Master of Medicine and the projected esoteric clinic with her husband in the role of Dr. Taverner.

The inside story of the confrontation between the Christian Mystic Lodge of the Theosophical Society of which she was president, and Bishop Piggot of the Liberal Catholic church, over the Star in the East movement and Krishnamurti. Also her group's experience of the magical conflict with Moina MacGregor Mathers.

How she and her husband befriended the young Israel Regardie, were present at his initiation into the Hermes Temple of the Stella Matutina, and suffered a second ejection from the Golden Dawn on his subsequent falling out with it.

Her renewed and highly secret contact with her old Golden Dawn teacher Maiya Tranchell-Hayes and their development of the esoteric side of the Arthurian legends.

Her peculiar and hitherto unknown work in policing the occult jurisdiction of the Master for whom she worked which brought her into unlikely contact with occultists such as Aleister Crowley.

Nor does the remarkable story end with her physical death for, through the mediumship of Margaret Lumley Brown and others, continued contacts with Dion Fortune have been reported over subsequent years.

ISBN 1-870450-50-7

LIVING MAGICAL ARTS
By R.J. Stewart

Living Magical Arts is founded upon the author's practical experience of the Western Magical Traditions, and contains specific teachings from within a living and long established initiatory line of British, French, and Russian esoteric tradition.

Living Magical Arts offers a new and clear approach to the philosophy and practice of magic for the 21st century, stripping away the accumulated nonsense found in many repetitive publications, and re-stating the art for contemporary use. This book offers a coherent illustrated set of magical techniques for individual or group use, leading to profound changes of consciousness and subtle energy. Magical arts are revealed as an enduring system of insight into human and universal consciousness, combining a practical spiritual psychology (long predating materialist psychology) with an effective method of relating to the physical world. Many of the obscure aspects of magical work are clarified, with insights into themes such as the origins of magical arts, working with subtle forces, partaking of esoteric traditions, liberating sexual energies, magical effects upon the world of nature, and the future potential and development of creative magic.

ISBN 1 870450 61 2

PRINCIPLES OF ESOTERIC HEALING
By Dion Fortune. Edited and arranged by Gareth Knight

One of the early ambitions of Dion Fortune along with her husband Dr Thomas Penry Evans was to found a clinic devoted to esoteric medicine, along the lines that she had fictionally described in her series of short stories *The Secrets of Dr. Taverner*. The original Dr. Taverner was her first occult teacher Dr. Theodore Moriarty, about whom she later wrote: "if there had been no Dr. Taverner there would have been no Dion Fortune!"

Shortly after their marriage in 1927 she and Dr. Evans began to receive a series of inner communications from a contact whom they referred to as the Master of Medicine. Owing to the pressure of all their other work in founding an occult school the clinic never came to fruition as first intended, but a mass of material was gathered in the course of their little publicised healing work, which combined esoteric knowledge and practice with professional medical expertise.

Most of this material has since been recovered from scattered files and reveals a fascinating approach to esoteric healing, taking into account the whole human being. Health problems are examined in terms of their physical, etheric, astral, mental or spiritual origination, along with principles of esoteric diagnosis based upon the structure of the Qabalistic Tree of Life. The function and malfunction of the psychic centres are described along with principles for their treatment by conventional or alternative therapeutic methods, with particular attention paid to the aura and the etheric double. Apart from its application to the healing arts much of the material is of wider interest for it demonstrates techniques for general development of the psychic and intuitive faculties apart from their more specialised use in assisting diagnosis.

ISBN 1 870450 85 X

PYTHONESS The Life & Work of Margaret Lumley Brown
By Gareth Knight

Margaret Lumley Brown was a leading member of Dion Fortune's Society of the Inner Light, taking over many of Dion Fortune's functions after the latter's death in 1946. She raised the arts of seership to an entirely new level and has been hailed with some justification as the finest medium and psychic of the 20th century. Although she generally sought anonymity in her lifetime her work was the source of much of the inner teachings of the Society from 1946 to 1961 and provided much of the material for Gareth Knight's *The Secret Tradition in Arthurian Legend* and *A Practical Guide to Qabalistic Symbolism*.

Gathered here is a four part record of the life and work of this remarkable woman. Part One presents the main biographical details largely as revealed by herself in an early work *Both Sides of the Door* an account of the frightening way in which her natural psychism developed as a consequence of experimenting with an ouija board in a haunted house. Part Two consists of articles written by her on such subjects as Dreams, Elementals, the Faery Kingdom, Healing and Atlantis, most of them commissioned for the legendary but short lived magazine *New Dimensions*. Part Three provides examples of her mediumship as Archpythoness of her occult fraternity with trance addresses on topics as diverse as Elemental Contacts, Angels and Archangels, Greek and Egyptian gods, and the Holy Grail. Part Four is devoted to the occult side of poetry, with some examples of her own work which was widely published in her day.

Gareth Knight was a colleague and friend of Margaret Lumley Brown in their days in the Society of the Inner Light together, to whom in later years she vouchsafed her literary remains, some esoteric memorabilia, and the privilege of being her literary executor.

ISBN 1 870450 75 2